THE
GOLDEN AGE
OF TRAVEL

Thomas Cook

THE GOLDEN AGE OF TRAVEL

The Romantic Years
of Tourism in Images
from the
Thomas Cook Archives

Andrew Williamson

Published by

Thomas Cook Publishing
PO Box 227
Thorpe Wood
Peterborough
PE3 6PU
United Kingdom

ISBN 1 900341 33 6

Managing Editor
Deborah Parker

Copy Editor
Leyla Davies

Additional research
Paul Smith, Jill Lomer and Joy Hooper,
Thomas Cook Archives

Cover and text design
Wenham Arts

Layout and additional design
Tina West

Typeset in
Berkeley Book and Palatino
using QuarkXPress for Windows

Repro and imagesetting
Pindar plc, Preston

Printed in Great Britain by
Pindar plc, Preston

Design for endpapers taken from interior of a sleeping tent (see page 21) used during the Holy Land tours conducted in the latter half of the 19th century

*T*o

Of course, I do
not object to two
or three
interruptions.
When a man is in
the full swing of
his work these
little things do not
affect him. Eight
or ten or twenty
interruptions
retard
composition.

Mark Twain
to Rudyard Kipling
in Kipling's
'From Sea to Sea'

CONTENTS

PREFACE

ABOUT THE PICTURES IN THIS BOOK

The ephemera of Thomas Cook's business, the pamphlets, posters and brochures, were not designed to survive for posterity. They were printed and published to promote and advertise upcoming tours, publicise new destinations and inform Cook's millions of customers worldwide. Their task completed, most were never seen again; thankfully a random selection survived and found their way into the custody of the Thomas Cook Archives. It is from this unrivalled window on the history of travel that all the pictures in this book have been taken.

Time and constant use have taken their toll on the tangible fragments of the Thomas Cook story that survive: tour brochures are creased and torn, newsletters printed on cheap paper have faded and illustrations have lost their lustre. In particular, very few of the early advertisements for Cook's services remain and those that do are either badly damaged or plain and visually unappealing. The majority of the images selected for this book therefore date from the second half of Cook's first century in business. In many cases, the illustrations originally appeared in black and white. Images in this book that have subsequently been coloured are indicated in the captions opposite these images. In most cases this was the result of a project begun in 1991, the 150th anniversary of Cook's first excursion. The work was carried out by Wally Doughty, a retired employee who had previously created window displays at the Berkeley Street store.

Thomas Cook's later fame obscures the difficulties he frequently faced in the early years of his excursion business. He organised his first tour of Ireland in 1849 and yet six years later the Irish railways announced their decision not to deal with Cook any more or to accept his tickets. It was to be a further 17 years before he again sent his customers to the Emerald Isle.

The pictures by themselves provide fascinating examples of the diversity and development of travel imagery in this golden age. They have also been carefully chosen to allow the accompanying text to explore as fully as possible the evolution of Cook's and the range of services and destinations on offer to its clients. Each accompanying commentary has deliberately been written as a stand-alone piece and therefore there is occasionally some factual repetition.

The final image, entitled 'To the Moon and Beyond', was specially commissioned for this book and was drawn by Patrick MacAllister.

WHAT'S IN A NAME?

By their very nature, the commentaries in this book move freely backwards and forwards through the history of the travel agency founded by Thomas Cook. This presents a constant dilemma of nomenclature: what to call the firm and how to distinguish the founder from the business that he created.

In the early years of Thomas Cook the man was the company. The two were synonymous, even when he hired others to assist him. Changes in direction, new initiatives and fresh ideas were first and foremost his responsibility. In 1864 Thomas's son, John Mason Cook, began working for his father full time. This was formally recognised in 1871 when a partnership was formed and the name was changed accordingly to Thomas Cook and Son. Cooks, be it father, son or grandsons, remained at the helm of the company until its sale to Wagons-Lit in 1928. Along the way it acquired limited-liability status and thus, from 1924, the new designation of Thos Cook & Son Ltd. In 1974, by which time the company was owned by a consortium comprising Midland Bank, Trust House Forte and the Automobile Association, the name came full circle and the company was rechristened Thomas Cook.

Throughout the period covered by this book the firm, whether it was in reality no more than the man himself, a partnership or a limited company employing thousands worldwide, was universally referred to simply as Cook's. I have therefore adopted this handy catch-all phrase regardless of the period under discussion.

There is another interesting terminology issue connected with Cook's. Right up until the 1970s, Cook's never referred to the people paying for its services as customers. They were termed passengers or even travellers, but never customers. They did, however, do everything that this term now implies. They bought Cook's tourist tickets, they took its tours and sought its advice. I have therefore used 'customer' freely in the text – hopefully without offence!

A NOTE ON PRICES
Exchange Rates

Numismatists' heaven is historians' hell. The golden age of travel is littered with obscure coins, long-forgotten currencies and strange-sounding monetary units that make hazardous the task of comparing prices. Among the more colourful coins in circulation in Europe in this period were the Napoleon, Isabelino, Frederick and Imperial, not to mention the *medio duro, skilling, thaler, scudi, crazia* and *kreutzer*. Britain's pre-decimal currency was equally tortuous: one English pound (known as a sovereign) was divided into 20 shillings (20s) and each shilling was worth 12 pence (abbreviated to the letter d, from the Latin *denarius*). A guinea, a common denomination for quoting prices, was equal to one pound and one shilling.

Whether due to genuine error or attempted fraud, the great array of foreign coinage caused even contemporary travellers a good deal of trouble. Thomas Cook confessed: 'we have ourselves been more than once caught by the "mistake" of accepting a sovereign for a napoleon, and being allowed for it twenty francs instead of twenty-five. And "mistakes" apart, it is a custom at most Bureau windows to allow twenty-three or twenty-four francs for a sovereign. We once had a severe contest with a clerk, who unblushingly and seemingly quite professionally, refused to give more than twenty-two francs for a sovereign'.

The redeeming feature of this multiplicity of coinage was its constant value. Throughout the life of Thomas Cook and his son, exchange rates varied very little, bringing a sense of stability and constancy to global travel. High-denomination coins often circulated freely between different countries. Only with the economic crises after World War I did this stability deteriorate, as illustrated by Britain's decision to leave the gold standard and Germany's ruinous hyperinflation.

All the prices given in this book are contemporary. The following typical pre-World War I exchange rates are given as a guide to their relative value in other currencies:

$£1$ = US $4.84
  = 25 francs (Belgium, French or Swiss)
  = 25 Italian lire
  = 25 Greek drachmas
  = 20 German marks
  = 10 Austrian florins
  = 1 Japanese yen
  = 13 Indian rupees

PRICES AND PAY

Knowing the cost of a Cook's tour or a sleeper on the Orient Express in a range of the world's major currencies is one thing; comparing it to today's prices is quite another. Social and technological changes have made this process notoriously difficult. A Victorian policeman, for example, earned less than half the wage of an train driver, while early cars were largely hand-built and were considered a luxury item.

By the 1880s the majority of Cook's business came from the sale of tickets to independent travellers. But conducted tours, by 'relieving the traveller of all petty troubles and annoyances inseparable from any journey', remained a distinctive feature of each year's programme.

Prices during Thomas Cook's lifetime stayed remarkably constant and in many cases even fell. Consequently, it is not unusual to find the cost of one of the firm's tours remaining unchanged over half a century, or even becoming cheaper as a result of economies of scale and improved technology. Price increases since this period have not been uniform. On average, a pint of beer in 1914 cost 2fid and a pack of cigarettes 4d, compared with £1.38 and £2.39 respectively in 1994. A double room at the Savoy Hotel in London on the eve of World War I cost £1 1s a night, compared with £195 (plus the inevitable VAT) 80 years later. Inflation had pushed up the price of a basic meal in the hotel's restaurant from 7s 6d to £31. Over this same period, a first-class return train ticket from London to Manchester has gone up from £2 9s to £130.

The annual pay increase was unheard of in Cook's day and salaries, while rising, did so only gradually. In 1914, the lowest paid workers, such as agricultural labourers, earned less than a pound a week, compared with up to £2 for the 'labour aristocracy'. A senior clerk could typically expect to earn up to £200 a year, an amount which bought a middle-class lifestyle with money enough to employ a servant at home and to qualify for income tax. Male elementary school teachers, in comparison, earned an average of £127 in 1914. An MP's salary in those days was £400 per annum and the prime minister received £5000.

ACKNOWLEDGEMENTS

The one internationally acceptable currency that an author has to repay the debt of gratitude owed to all those whose generous assistance helps bring a book to life is a mention in the list of acknowledgements. I would therefore like to cash in my IOUs and proffer my heartfelt thanks to: Ruth Binney and Alison Moss for setting the ball rolling; Nicky Thompson for persevering against the odds; past and present custodians of the Thomas Cook Archives – Paul Smith, Jill Lomer, Joy Hooper and Fiona Kelly – for welcoming me so warmly to their Aladdin's cave; Barry for the slippers up Majuba Hill; and Bob for an item not dissimilar to a palanquin. Until the next time.

THE GOLDEN AGE OF TRAVEL

INTRODUCTION

We may live without poetry, music and art,
We may live without conscience and live
without heart,
We may live without friends,
We may live without books,
But civilized man cannot live without Cook's.

Robert Bulwer-Lytton,
1st earl of Lytton (1831–91)

*Not until he was 32
did Thomas Cook
(1808–92), founder
of the world-famous
travel agency that
still bears his name,
take his first small
step in a career that
would change the
face of global travel
forever.*

THE INDISPENSABLE MR COOK

It is hard to comprehend today, with hundreds of competing holiday providers, how far the firm of Thomas Cook & Son dominated the world travel scene during the golden age of travel. Thomas Cook was not the first person to organise a railway excursion, to publish a guidebook or even arrange a conducted tour, but his name became a byword for quality and service in all aspects of travel. It was jokingly claimed that Thomas Cook & Son stood alongside the Roman Catholic Church and the Prussian army as one of the most efficient organisations of the Victorian age.

By 1891, the firm's golden jubilee, Thomas Cook & Son had 84 offices spanning the globe. This one, located in the grounds of Shepheard's Hotel in Cairo, Egypt, opened in 1872.

Long before the term had been coined, Cook's offices were the one-stop travel shop *par excellence*. They provided everything the traveller could possibly require: holiday packages and accommodation, conducted tours, traveller's cheques, guidebooks, timetables, travel insurance, visa and passport applications, endless free advice and, above all, tickets to a seemingly inexhaustible list of destinations over innumerable routes and combinations of conveyance. By the 1930s, the firm of Thos Cook & Son Ltd provided every imaginable service from translation and typing, baggage storage and forwarding, to house hunting and a shopping service, banking services and the placing of children in private schools.

Cook's infiltrated the very fabric of people's lives and tourists' invocation of its name had miraculous results: bedrooms suddenly became available, staff fell over backwards to oblige and previously impossible tasks were performed without delay. When once a steamer was kept waiting by the antics of a tiresome spinster, an exasperated passenger threatened her with the ultimate sanction: 'Madam, you are an impertinent old woman; I shall report you to the Captain, the purser and Cook's in London'.

Cook's universality was also beyond question. There was no corner of the globe untouched by Cook's organisation or where its influence did not extend. This is well illustrated by a contemporary cartoon. A cannibal chief, surrounded by his fierce warriors, is seen untying his harried victim with the words: 'Why didn't you say before that you were from Cook's – I'm their local agent'. By the 1930s, Cook's was making travel arrangements for over five million clients annually, more than twice the combined total of every other travel agent.

This book examines the golden age of travel through the life of a hard-working and pious temperance advocate from a small village near Leicester, and the world-famous travel agency that he founded.

The fruits of an inventive mind. Thomas Cook's travel innovations included a prepaid hotel coupon (below) and an early type of traveller's cheque (middle).

THE GOLDEN AGE OF TRAVEL

The golden age of travel is a nebulous term. It is both disparate and lacking in any set demarcation, and yet detailed definition is somehow superfluous so legendary are its icons: the Orient Express, Train Bleu and Flying Scotsman, *Île de France*, *Lusitania* and the ill-fated *Titanic*. By association, this title can be extended from the gracious means of transport to the luxurious palace hotels waiting at journey's end and on to encompass the whole Victorian and Edwardian travel experience. It covers everything from a week spent under canvas on African safari to a tour of the ruins of past civilisations in the jungle of southeast Asia.

The application of steam power to the means of transport at the beginning of the 19th century revolutionised travel and ushered in this halcyon age; the arrival of the jet plane heralded its end. The perception of this era as a golden age is therefore tinged with a sentimentality for the lost days of steam trains and ocean liners. Regardless of the reality, the term conjures up an image of a more sedate and leisurely time, when travel was a strictly first-class affair, full of liveried attendants, polite conversation and gracious dining. Travel, in contrast to the depersonalised voyages of today, was always tinged with a sense of adventure and camaraderie. The very fact that journey times were measured in days rather than hours helps give this age its peculiar allure.

Ironically, the constant technological advances that brought about this golden age, making railways and ships faster, safer and more comfortable, also hastened its demise. The generation that crossed Europe on the Orient Express and sailed to America on the *Mauretania* and *Normandie* were in turn quick to embrace the automobile and the aeroplane. These new members of the transport family made their own contribution to the legend of the golden age – with names such as Rolls-Royce and Mercedes-Benz, Douglas and De Havilland – but they also irrevocably changed the way people travelled.

World War II proved a watershed in the story of the golden age of travel and the arrival of the jet plane shortly afterwards

For travelling in style up the Nile, Cook's fleet of luxury steamers was unsurpassed. The Rameses, *seen here in front of the Temple of Karnak at Luxor, was built in 1887. It provided accommodation for up to 77 passengers, first class only, had a top speed of 11 mph and its own bakehouse on board.*

signalled its end. The transatlantic liners were taken out of service and the sleek steam locomotives sold for scrap. But despite these great changes, the names of those who are synonymous with this golden age have not been forgotten: Pullman, Cunard, Ritz and Thomas Cook, a Baptist-preacher-turned-excursion-organiser from Leicester.

Thomas Cook's rise to prominence was part and parcel of this golden age; the growth of the eponymous firm he founded was inextricably linked with the development of the train and steamship. Cook acted as agent for all the world's principal rail and ship companies, selling their tickets in exchange for a small commission. He negotiated special rates with them and was able to provide his customers with combined tickets that traversed the networks of any number of different principals.

Cook's provides a unifying force, a common identity that this golden age otherwise lacks. It acted as a link between the multitude of different liners, luxury trains, hotels and travel opportunities. Regardless of whether the traveller wished to take a leisurely trip up the Nile, tour Europe's cultural gems or explore the Amazon rain forest, the offices of Thomas Cook & Son could make all the necessary arrangements.

FROM MELBOURNE TO MARKET HARBOROUGH (1808–40)

John and Elizabeth Cook, who lived at 9 Quick Close in the village of Melbourne, Derbyshire, England, named their first child after Elizabeth's father. Thomas Perkins, who had died when Elizabeth was only a child, had been co-pastor of Melbourne General Baptist Church and well respected in the local community. His grandson, Thomas Cook, was born at five o'clock in the morning of 22 November 1808. His name was as unexceptional as his upbringing.

Thomas's parents, both committed Baptists, instilled in their son their belief in hard work and a strong faith that was to serve him well in the course of his life. John Cook sadly died when Thomas was only three years old, but his mother, who remarried later that same year, ensured that Thomas was provided with a basic education. As was usual in a family of modest means, Thomas Cook began his working life early. His first job, at the age of 10, was as an assistant to a local market gardener for a wage of sixpence a week. Four years later, he was fortunate enough to secure an apprenticeship, with John Pegg, and spent five years learning to be a cabinet maker.

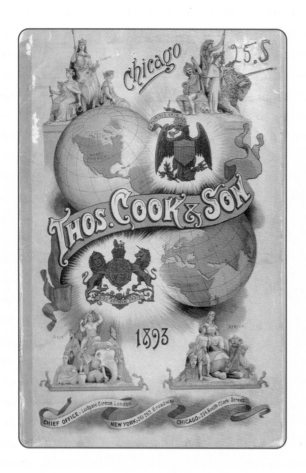

By the time of Chicago's World's Fair in 1893, a tardy celebration of the 400th anniversary of Columbus's discovery of America, Cook's not only made travel arrangements for visitors but also had its own stand, which displayed models of Cook's Nile Steamers.

Cook's, official agents to steamship companies great and small alike, was there to help whether a customer wished to cross the Atlantic in state-room luxury, emigrate cheaply to Australia or go island hopping in the Pacific.

Thomas Cook was now assured of a secure livelihood and a settled future seemed certain. Instead, following his baptism in February 1826, Thomas turned his attention to preaching. Over the next few years he toured the region as a village evangelist, preaching the word of God and distributing pamphlets, and occasionally being forced to practise his trade when funds ran low.

In 1832, Thomas Cook moved to Adam and Eve Street in Market Harborough (population 2272), a few miles southeast of Leicester. It was here, influenced by Francis Beardsall, the local Baptist minister, that Cook made a decision that was to fundamentally alter the course of his life. On New Year's Day 1833, he took the temperance pledge. Although he abstained initially only from spirits, and not beer, Thomas's nonconformist background and missionary zeal made him an ideal recruit to the teetotal cause. He threw himself wholeheartedly into the fight against liquor, organising meetings, holding processions and inveighing against demon drink, which he described as 'Death's Prime Minister'.

On 3 March 1833, amid this flurry of activity, Thomas Cook found time to marry Marianne Mason. When a son was born on 13 January 1834, Thomas named him John Mason in honour of the grandfather he had never known and his wife's family. Cook later admitted that temperance was the 'guiding star of my public as well as private life'. His supportive spouse helped the family finances by taking in temperance travellers at their home, while her husband took up yet another new profession: he began publishing tracts, such as the *Temperance Messenger* and *The Children's Temperance Magazine*. Ironically, it was Marianne who first decided to espouse complete abstinence and only in December 1836 did Thomas follow her.

On 22 November 1840, Thomas Cook celebrated his 32nd birthday. He could look back with satisfaction on a long and varied working life, oblivious of the momentous event that was soon to redefine his existence.

FROM LOUGHBOROUGH TO LEICESTER (1841–65)

Thomas Cook recounted later in life the exact moment when he decided to organise his first excursion. The date was 9 June 1841. While walking to Leicester from his home, a distance of some 14 miles, an idea suddenly seized him: 'What a glorious thing it would be if the newly-developed powers of railways and locomotion could be made subservient to the promotion of temperance!'

The chance to put this noble philosophy into practice was already close at hand. A gathering of temperance supporters in nearby Loughborough had been arranged for Monday, 5 July 1841. Groups from the surrounding region had been invited to attend. Cook therefore suggested organising a special excursion train to convey the contingent from Leicester. This idea was enthusiastically welcomed by his local temperance society and a special, half-price fare of one-shilling was negotiated with the Midland Railway. Despite the short notice, Cook threw himself wholeheartedly into promoting this new venture, printing posters, selling tickets and drumming up support.

The *Leicester Chronicle* reported the scene on the day of departure. 'On getting to the railway-station on the London-road, we found a large crowd of Teetotallers gathered together, in waiting for the "special train" . . . They were accompanied by an excellent band, and were headed by their district officers and flags'. Thomas, accompanied by his seven-year-old son, was among this party of some 500 who set off from Leicester in open-topped carriages amid much cheering and excitement. They were met at Loughborough by a brass band and marched in triumph to a local park where food was provided, games held and a stream of speeches followed. The event was a great success and marks the official founding of Cook's world-famous travel agency.

In September of 1841, Thomas Cook moved his family to Leicester, where he established a printing and bookselling business. His next major undertaking was in 1845, when he

organised a pleasure trip to Liverpool and North Wales. Cook had to negotiate with three different railway companies, but he was finally able to offer first- and second-class tickets for the trip priced at 15s and 10s respectively. Cook, with his usual meticulous preparation, not only printed his own posters and advertisements, but also researched and wrote a *Handbook of the Trip to Liverpool* to accompany the visit.

In 1846, spurred on by the success of his latest venture, Cook escorted his first party to Scotland. Tours to the Highlands were to form the backbone of his excursion activities for the next 20 years, although he seized any opportunity that presented itself. The biggest of these was the

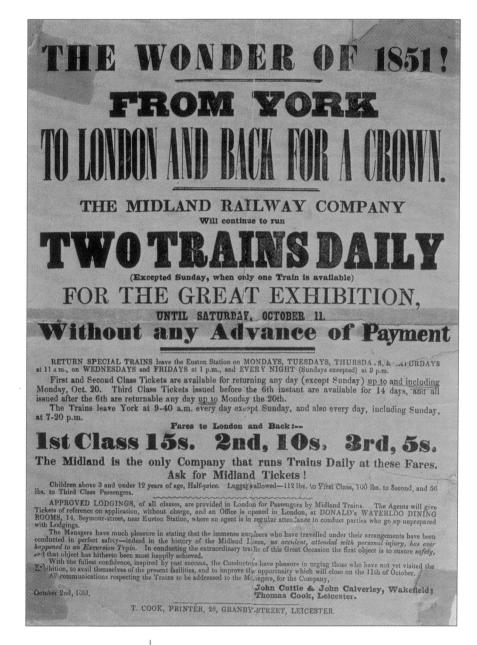

The first World's Fair, held in Hyde Park, London between May and October 1851, provided a welcome lift to Cook's fledgling business. In all he made travel arrangements for some 150,000 people to visit the Crystal Palace.

Great Exhibition of 1851 held in Hyde Park, London. Cook made travel arrangements for some 150,000 visitors to see this celebration of man's achievements. Other one-off events followed, such as the Manchester Fine Arts Exhibition, and the French decision to hold their own World's Fair in Paris in 1855 prompted Thomas Cook to arrange his first tour to the Continent. He led his party to Paris via the major sights of Belgium and the Rhine and eight years later, when the railway companies put a ban on excursions north of the border, he returned to Europe with his first combined tour to Paris and Switzerland. The next year, 1864, Cook went a step further and began running tours across the Alps into Italy.

Thomas Cook's business was now at a crucial juncture. He took advantage of the success of his forays into Europe and, in the pivotal year of 1865, opened his first London office at 98 Fleet Street. John Mason Cook, who had finally joined his father full time the previous year, ran the office with the help of one clerk and an office boy, while Thomas crossed the Atlantic to explore the opportunities that awaited him in the New World.

The Slow Rise to Fame

The universality of Cook's organisation by the end of Queen Victoria's reign belies the slow start that the firm's founder made. There was nothing inevitable about Cook's rise to prominence in the aftermath of his 1841 excursion. In fact, the man who is credited with the foundation of modern tourism showed a marked hesitancy in pursuing his new calling.

It was to be five years before Cook got as far as Scotland and 14 years before he crossed the Channel. It was only in 1854, at the ripe old age of 45, that Thomas Cook decided to give up general printing and devote himself to tourism. Cook did not set out to establish a worldwide travel agency. He saw travel as a means of social improvement and he consequently put philanthropy before profit. His business survived on the tiniest of margins and this reason alone necessitated his cautious expansion.

The Travel Pioneer

The coming of the railways made large-scale organised travel possible. These two industries evolved side by side and learnt from each other, though not without the inevitable growing

Full-length dresses and a protective parasol were de rigueur for a Victorian lady, even when tackling a Swiss glacier. Here a tour party makes its way across the Mer de Glace near Chamonix in the 1880s.

pains. Thomas Cook initially had great difficulty persuading the railway and steamship companies to accept his business. Their reluctance stemmed both from a wariness about embracing the new excursion culture and also from a belief that they could avoid paying a commission to a travel agent and organise the excursions themselves. This problem was particularly acute in 1855, when Cook organised his first European venture. The companies that controlled the shorter cross-Channel routes rebuffed his overtures and he was forced to take his party through the port of Antwerp in Belgium. Only when they realised the profit that Cook's patronage offered did the transport companies welcome his custom.

By setting the standards and establishing the practises of the modern travel agent, Cook earned his right to be considered a pioneer. There were few, if any, precedents for much of what Cook did, and so he had to learn on his own and make his own rules as he went along. He frequently found his tours as instructive as his charges, learning from his mistakes and seeing gaps in service that needed filling.

On Cook's early tours, for instance, participants paid only their fares in advance. Other expenses, such as accommodation or sightseeing trips, had to be divided among the party as the tour progressed. Gradually, Cook developed a pre-payment method for hotels and every other conceivable tourist convenience, he introduced his own form of traveller's cheque and freed tourists from the need to travel in groups. It is hard to understand just how daunting a prospect foreign travel was before Cook simplified and cheapened the process.

A Very Personal Travel Agent

Thomas Cook's personal approach to the business of travel was initially necessitated by the small scale of his fledgling enterprise. In naming the firm after himself, there was no attempt at aggrandisement: in the early years, Thomas Cook was the business. Its successes, and failures, were based on his own hard work and the good reputation that he laboured to establish.

Any destination to which Thomas Cook intended to send his tourists, he preferred to visit himself beforehand. He would laboriously collect information, check arrangements and undertake the arduous negotiations with transport companies and hoteliers. The first guidebooks which Cook's published were written by him as a result of this intensive study. Tour members frequently found themselves conducted by *the* Mr Cook; he also found time to edit the *Excursionist* and much of its purple prose flowed from his pen.

In many ways, Cook's early tours resembled a family outing rather than a commercial undertaking. He would rely on

A Cook's ticket was a passport to a world of adventure. Contained in a distinctive green case, it provided the holder with access to destinations across the world and to the services of Cook's worldwide network of uniformed representatives and interpreters.

members of his party to translate for him and a strong sense of camaraderie developed as they took meals together and shared accommodation.

An Unlikely Revolutionary

Travel, exemplified by the Grand Tour of the 18th century, had traditionally been the preserve of the male members of the upper classes. Thomas Cook, motivated by a genuine desire to raise the condition of the working classes and provide an alternative to the evil of the ale house, helped make travel universally affordable. He organised a wide range of cheap day trips to seaside towns, special events and places of historical interest. His longer tours appealed to the middle classes, to teachers, doctors, vicars and merchants, who had the time and money to travel further afield.

Women, too, had traditionally been excluded from travelling. The reasons were concerns about safety and the ever-present question of propriety. The idea of an unmarried woman travelling alone was frowned upon, which inevitably limited women's freedom of movement. Cook referred to himself as a 'travelling chaperone' and by offering 'personally conducted' tours whose moral character was beyond reproach, he provided a safe and socially acceptable environment for unaccompanied women. His tours frequently attracted more women than men and he can be rightly credited with furthering the cause of women's emancipation.

Ludgate Circus: an address familiar to travellers for over half a century. It was chosen as the site of Cook's worldwide headquarters in 1873 because, joked the Excursionist, *'a jocular friend of ours wrote some time back saying he had been making a very careful calculation, and as a result he had discovered that the exact "centre of civilisation" was under the lamp-post at Ludgate Circus'.*

FROM IRRITANT TO INSTITUTION (1866–91)

After quarter of a century as an 'excursion and tourist manager', Thomas Cook finally found his business starting to prosper, and with this success the firm began its transformation from an object of ridicule into an indispensable institution. His son now took a growing role in the administration of the business, while Thomas, his energy still undiminished, acted as a roving ambassador, travelling far and wide and laying the groundwork for Cook's expansion into new regions.

The first success was John Mason Cook's conducted tour of the United States in 1866. This was followed by the inaugural tour to Egypt and the Holy Land under Thomas's supervision in 1869 and then a world tour that took Thomas around the globe via the United States, Japan and India. As more and more people began to travel, Cook continued to make the process easier: 1868 saw the launch of the firm's hotel coupon scheme; next came the first monthly edition of *Cook's Continental Time Tables* in 1873; the next year the first Cook's traveller's cheque made its debut; and in 1878 a Banking and Exchange Department was established.

John Mason Cook's contribution was recognised in 1871, when he became a partner and the firm was officially redesignated Thomas Cook & Son. He arranged the move to a new London head office while his father was on his round-the-world tour, and soon there were offices from Brisbane to Bombay. In 1879, while his father retired to Leicester, John took over sole responsibility for the firm. He was now free to follow his own path, eschewing what he saw as Thomas's lack of business sense and courting a wealthier class of patron. This

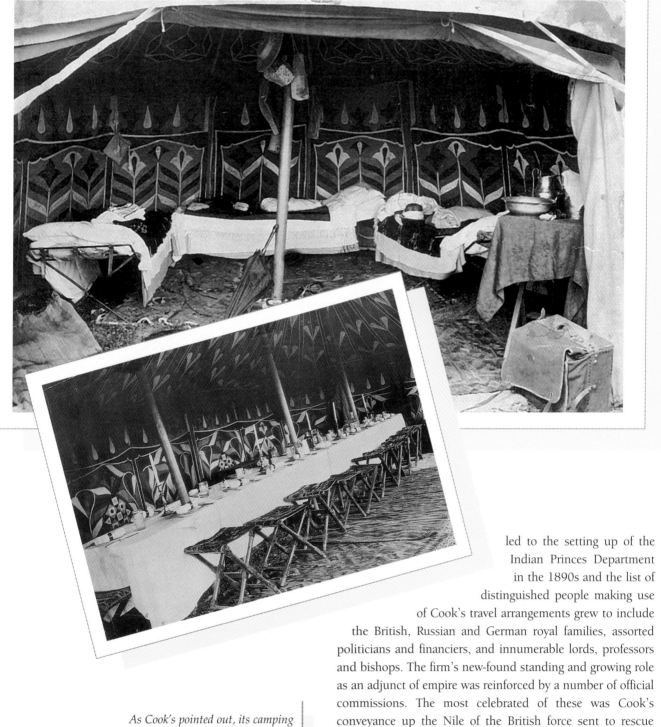

As Cook's pointed out, its camping arrangements for tours of the Holy Land were 'the best that practical experience and unstinted expenditure can possibly provide'. A typical sleeping tent (top) accommodated 'three travellers of the same sex' and included 'candlesticks, water bottle and glasses, carpets for the floors, chairs, [and] toilet utensils'. Meals in the dining tent (below) were served on 'dinner and tea services [the] same as in an hotel'.

led to the setting up of the Indian Princes Department in the 1890s and the list of distinguished people making use of Cook's travel arrangements grew to include the British, Russian and German royal families, assorted politicians and financiers, and innumerable lords, professors and bishops. The firm's new-found standing and growing role as an adjunct of empire was reinforced by a number of official commissions. The most celebrated of these was Cook's conveyance up the Nile of the British force sent to rescue General Gordon from Khartoum.

The firm of Thomas Cook & Son celebrated its golden jubilee in 1891 with an elaborate dinner held in the Whitehall Room at the Metropole Hotel in London and hosted by John Mason Cook. He was able to reflect with pride on half a century of progress. The firm, from its simple beginnings as a one-man show, had grown into a worldwide force, with 84 offices, 85 agencies and 2692 staff. It now issued over three and a half million tickets annually and could claim with satisfaction to be the authorised agent of every steamship company and railway line of repute in the world.

The imposing countenance of John Mason Cook (1834–99) was described by a contemporary: 'Tall and strongly knit, he stands erect and firm on his legs to-day, though his beard is snow-white and his round forehead is bare. His white eyebrows bristle resolutely over just the eyes that such a man ought to have – eyes that look out of their sockets like a gun out of a port.'

Like Father, like Son

In many ways, John Mason Cook was a chip off the old block. He abstained from alcohol throughout his life and was a determined and wilful man imbued with a rapacious appetite for hard work. He too set up as a printer and gained his travel expertise from personal experience. However, his approach to work, and the finances of the firm in particular, put him at odds with his father.

John, who possessed an excellent business sense, was frustrated by his father's lax attitude to profit. John believed his hard work in building up the firm's fortunes were being frittered away by Thomas's more altruistic leanings. The two clashed frequently on this issue and, after the establishment of the London office, John increasingly dominated the firm and moulded it to his own personality. He even bundled his father into an unwanted early retirement at the end of 1878 and relations between them became strained towards the end of Thomas's life.

This unfitting end to Thomas Cook's long career proved to be exactly the tonic that the firm needed. The timing of John's ascendancy was ideal and he was able to build on Thomas's

solid yet barely profitable foundations and turn the company into a global force. His personal involvement rivalled that of his father and his obsession with detail meant that nothing escaped his attention. He frequently worked 18 hours a day during the summer season, managing the office in London, keeping the company accounts and between 1865 and 1873 he still found time to travel up to 53,000 miles and spend more than 100 nights away from home each year. He was as demanding of others as he was of himself, insisting, for example, that the letters, up to 200 a day, which arrived at the Fleet Street office were answered by return of post.

John's efforts not only put the company on a sounder economic footing, but pushed it relentlessly into new regions, as far apart as Bosnia, Alaska and Morocco, supported by a truly international network of offices and representatives. He paid particular attention to the company's Egyptian operations, which he had been largely responsible for establishing, and after 1885 he spent every winter there.

John Mason Cook also introduced a new generation of Cooks to the travel business. He sent his three sons, Frank, Ernest and Thomas, as far afield as Australia, India and Egypt as his lieutenants, promoting the family business and helping to secure his gains.

Rich Man, Poor Man

Cook's tourists were initially treated with the same disdain that is today levelled at people on cheap package holidays to the sun spots of Europe. The fact that Thomas Cook was enabling a whole new class of people to travel to foreign climes that had once been the sole prerogative of the wealthy Grand Tourists made him the subject of much animosity. The charges levelled at him and his tour parties included vulgarity, ignorance and the spoiling of sites. He found himself the butt of many a joke and cartoonist's wit. But these same people, who had poured such scorn on Cook in the early years, lost no time in rushing to use his services once they realised the efficacy of his arrangements. Cook was now lauded as the 'patron saint' of travel, the Napoleon of excursions and 'conductor to the world'.

John Mason accelerated Cook's acceptance by the Establishment by deliberately setting out to woo the rich and the well known. In 1879, as part of this move upmarket, he announced: 'we have decided to reduce the numbers of our parties and keep them more manageable than they have hitherto been'. Lists of some of the distinguished individuals who had used Cook's services began to appear in company brochures.

One of Cook's Holy Land parties, its tents already pitched, poses for a picture after a day in the saddle. Twenty years after Thomas Cook led his first group to the Holy Land in 1869, Cook's offered six weeks in Palestine, with stops en route, for £166; one-month tours were available for £147.

William Gladstone, the great Liberal politician, viewed Thomas Cook as a kindred spirit in his efforts to improve people through travel and he considered Cook's travel system 'among the humanising contrivances of the age'. Rudyard Kipling spoke in glowing terms of 'the great J. M. [Cook] – the man with the iron mouth and the domed brow'. Mark Twain often used Cook's services and his praise was typically fulsome: 'Cook has made travel simple, easy and a pleasure. He will sell you a ticket to any place on the globe, or all the places, and give you all the time you need, and as much more besides; and it is good for all trains of its class, and its baggage is weighable at all hours . . . I recommend Cook's tickets and I do this without embarrassment, for I get no commission. I do not know Cook'.

Another grateful customer was Lord Randolph Churchill who travelled up the Nile with Cook's and whose son Winston, another Cook's customer, noted on his way to Omdurman with the British army: 'The versatile and ubiquitous Cook had undertaken the arrangements, as his name painted on everything clearly showed'. Oscar Wilde, during his exile in Paris, asked friends not to send financial support via registered mail, but instead to use Thomas Cook & Son who 'wire money like angels'.

The Evolving Travel Scene

Thomas Cook did not operate in a vacuum. He had rivals and competitors, some of whom got there before him, others whom he attacked for trying to 'obstruct our progress or to filch from us the just reward of our exertions'. These competitors came and went. One of the most persistent was Henry Gaze, who started in business in the 1850s but, like so many others, eventually fell by the wayside.

Travel agency was always a precarious business, especially in the early years when operators had to contend with seasonal fluctuations and the fickleness of public support. Margins were always small and there were not many people who were prepared to emulate Cook, putting in endless hard work for incredibly little financial reward.

Some seized the opportunity for quick returns or sprang up to meet temporary demand before disappearing as quickly as they had appeared. Even a modern-day travel giant such as American Express had no interest initially in Cook's line of business. Its president, James Fargo, expressed his disdain with the emphatic utterance: 'I will not have gangs of day trippers starting off from charabancs in front of our offices the way they do at Cooks'.

Unlike some of the more capricious Victorian operators, Cook's was the constant companion of the traveller. It grew and adapted as the demands and sophistication of the tourist changed, evolving from the provision of simple excursions, through guided tours to fully independent travel. As transport improved and new opportunities, such as the opening of the Suez Canal in 1869, presented themselves, Cook's was on hand to ease the passage of the travelling public.

FROM SON TO GRANDSONS (1891–1916)

In the space of less than seven years, Thomas Cook & Son lost both its founder and his son. Thomas died peacefully on

Thomas Cook's three grandsons, pictured here in the 1890s, inherited the family business after the untimely death of their father in 1899. It was sold to the operator of the famed Orient Express train in 1928.

*Loaded up and
ready to go: a
charabanc
waits to depart
outside one of
Cook's Berlin
agencies.*

18 July 1892 at the age of 83, leaving a modest estate valued at £2497 1s 6d. The next issue of the *Excursionist*, its borders draped in black as a mark of respect, paid tribute to this remarkable man: 'in private life he was one of the kindest of friends, and his public career furnishes a striking example of the success of a self-made man of cosmopolitan ideas and international friendships. It is difficult to estimate the amount of good produced by Mr. Thomas Cook's long and eminent labours'.

John Mason Cook's death in 1899 at the relatively young age of 65, due to its suddenness, was an even greater blow to the company. Exhausted by the work attendant on organising the Kaiser's expedition to the Holy Land, he caught dysentery and never fully recovered. He died at Mount Felix, his home in Walton-on-Thames, on 4 March, leaving an estate of £663,534, a tribute to his financial acumen. The *Excursionist* acknowledged his own unique contribution to the business's success: 'if the honour of originating the excursion system belongs to Mr. Thomas Cook the father, to John Mason Cook the son belongs the credit of having moulded it into what it is by his organising genius, his marvellous energy, and his tremendous capacity for work'.

With Cook and son gone, a third generation of the family stepped in to fill the gap. John's three sons, already experienced in the travel trade, were well equipped to carry on the family tradition. They in their turn were as different from their father as he was from his, but again the change of character suited the times. Cook's no longer required a pioneer or a workhorse, but sensible, undramatic leadership.

Thomas, the youngest of the three, was bought out by his brothers shortly after his father's death, Ernest settled for the reassuring routine of working in the Banking Department at

Ludgate Circus and so responsibility for the day-to-day running of the company fell to Frank. His more impersonal, bureaucratic and conservative style of management suited what was now a worldwide company. Under his guidance, Thomas Cook & Son reinforced its position as the world's leading travel agent and in the years leading up to World War I returned a respectable annual profit of over £86,000.

The company concentrated on doing what it did best: selling tickets and providing unrivalled travel services. It continued to offer increasingly elaborate and exotic tours for the wealthy, including excursions by motor car and trips to far-flung lands, and yet Cook's also arranged tickets for millions of far-more-prosaic journeys, such as a bank-holiday outing to the seaside, a week in the Lake District, or an independent tour of one of Europe's cultural centres.

The Great War caught Cook's as much by surprise as everyone else. The company was able to use its resources to send mail, via its office in neutral Amsterdam, to people living in enemy countries, but with all thoughts of leisure travel expelled it was forced to reduce its staff and suffered a loss of almost £250,000.

FROM COOKS TO CONFLICT (1916–41)

When the armistice was declared on 11 November 1918, things quickly returned to normal as people determined to make up for four lost years. Cook's took up where it had left off and soon the war time and its attendant hardships seemed little more than an unfortunate hiatus in the travel agent's continued prosperity.

Business boomed: the company issued its first air-travel brochure; the vogue for world cruises led Cook's to conduct several voyages aboard the Cunard liner *Franconia*; the discovery of Tutankhamen's tomb by Howard Carter in 1922 provided a considerable boost to the Egyptian business; and the 1926 move to a smart, spacious new headquarters in Berkeley Street capped a decade of success.

Then the bombshell hit. Frank and Ernest, custodians of the Cook legacy, announced in February 1928 their decision to sell the entire business to the Compagnie Internationale des Wagons-Lits, which operated most of Europe's luxury sleeping cars, including the Orient Express. The cost of almost three-quarters of a century of family toil was £3.5 million.

The sale took everyone by surprise. Many lamented the passing of the family connection and yet the onset of a global depression proved that the timing had been fortuitous. Thomas Cook would certainly have been glad that his family did not have to be part of the hard times that lay ahead. The worst year was 1931, when the annual six-figure profits of the 1920s were transformed into a loss of almost £200,000. The freehold of the newly completed London headquarters had to be sold, staff numbers were drastically cut back to 2544 and the company was even forced to dispose of the majority of the famed Nile fleet that John had laboured so hard to build up.

These sad events seemed to signal the end of the world that Cook and his son had known. Rampant inflation in countries such as Germany, and Britain's decision to come off the gold standard, heralded the end of the era of stable prices and constant exchange rates; growing nationalism and increasing military tension threatened to close the borders that Cook had worked so hard to break down; and the growing presence of the motor car and aeroplane cast a long shadow over the final years of Cook's first century in business.

The company did manage to recover by the end of the 1930s, only to be plunged into fresh crisis by the events of 1 September 1939, when German tanks started rolling across the Polish border. When France and the Low Countries fell the following spring, the Wagons-Lits headquarters in Paris and Brussels were taken over by the Germans and Cook's British

assets were requisitioned as enemy property. To save Cook 's from complete financial collapse in its centenary year, a deal was brokered and, fittingly, the organisation was sold to Britain's four mainline railway companies. The golden age of travel had come to an inglorious end.

The world had become a smaller place thanks to Cook's. Its uniformed representatives, instantly recognisable, were tangible proof of the firm's global presence.

IL VESUVIO
con
«FERROVIA»«FUNICOLARE»

1808	**Thomas Cook** is born on 22 November in the village of Melbourne, Derbyshire.
1819	The *Savannah* becomes the first ship to employ steam power in crossing the Atlantic, a journey that took 27 days and 11 hours.
1833	**Thomas Cook** signs a pledge of abstinence from ardent spirits at Market Harborough on New Year's Day.
1834	**Thomas's** son, **John Mason Cook**, is born on 13 January.
1837	Accession of **Queen Victoria** to the British throne and the founding of the Peninsular & Oriental Steam Navigation Company.
1839	**Samuel Cunard** establishes the British and North American Royal Mail Steam Packet Company, the first regular Atlantic steamship company.
1841	On 5 July, some 500 Temperance supporters travel from Leicester to Loughborough on **Thomas Cook's** first organised excursion. Return tickets cost one shilling.
1845	**Thomas Cook** arranges an excursion to Liverpool and North Wales, which departs on 4 August.
1846	**Cook** personally conducts the first of his many tours to Scotland.
1850	**César Ritz**, whose name becomes synonymous with luxury in the hotel world, is born in Niederwald, Switzerland.
1851	**Cook** transports an estimated 150,000 people from the Midlands to the Great Exhibition in Hyde Park. He also begins publishing the forerunner of *The Excursionist*.
1855	**Cook's** first tour on the Continent is hampered by the difficulty of securing rail concessions.

1862 Birth of **Frank Henry Cook**, the first of **John Mason's** five children. He has two more sons – **Ernest Edward** (born 1865) and **Thomas Albert** (known as **Bert**, born 1867) – and all three enter the family business.

1863 **Thomas** leads his first combined tour of Paris and Switzerland.

1864 **John Mason** abandons his own printing business to work full time for his father.

1865 **Cook** opens an office at 98 Fleet Street; **George Pullman** gets his big break when one of his luxury carriages is used to carry **Abraham Lincoln's** body from Washington DC to his birthplace in Springfield, Illinois.

1866 Following an investigatory tour by his father the previous year, **John Mason** conducts the firm's first tour to the United States and Canada.

1868 **Thomas Cook** introduces his hotel coupon scheme.

1869 **Thomas** travels to Egypt and Palestine at the head of party of about 30. He is invited to return in November to attend the opening of the Suez Canal.

1871 Thirty-one years after work began, the first locomotive finally passes through the Mount Cennis Tunnel linking France and Italy. **John Mason Cook** is made a partner in the family business and the firm's name is officially changed to **Thomas Cook & Son**.

1872 **Thomas** sets off on the company's first round-the-world tour.

1873 **Thomas Cook & Son** move to new, more spacious offices at Ludgate Circus. The first issue of *Cook's Continental Time Tables* is published.

1874 **Cook's** launches its Circular Note, an early form of traveller's cheque.

1879 **John** becomes the company's 'sole managing partner'.

1883 Inauguration of the Orient Express.

1884 John Mason transports the British relief force, sent to rescue **General Gordon** from Khartoum, and all its supplies up the Nile as far as Wadi Halfa.

1887 For six years **John Mason Cook**, at the behest of the Indian viceroy, organises the transport of Muslim faithful on the annual pilgrimage to Mecca. He also takes over the Mount Vesuvius funicular railway in Italy.

1892 **Thomas Cook** dies on 19 July at the age of 83.

1898 **John** organises **Kaiser Wilhelm II's** tour of the Holy Land.

John Mason Cook, recently returned from Palestine, dies suddenly on 4 March at the age of 65. **Frank** and **Ernest** take over the running of the business, which now enters a golden period when it dominates travel across the globe.

1899

Cook's organises its first motor tour.

1900

Orville Wright completes the first sustained aeroplane flight.

1903

The Trans-Siberian Railway, at 5800 miles the longest in the world, is completed.

1905

The *Mauretania*, which holds the blue ribbon for the fastest Atlantic crossing between 1907 and 1929, is launched.

1906

The firm's Inclusive Independent Tours are launched in England. This innovation provides the unaccompanied traveller with an all-inclusive fare and a planned itinerary paid for in advance.

1907

Henry Ford introduces his Model T car.

1908

The 'unsinkable' *Titanic* goes down off Newfoundland on the night of 14 April, with the loss of over 1500 lives.

1912

Cook's rescues tourists stranded in enemy territory on the outbreak of World War I in August, and runs a mail service to enemy countries through its offices in neutral countries. **Thomas (Bert) Cook**, the founder's grandson, dies unexpectedly on 5 September at the age of 47. His brother **Frank** dies in 1931 and **Ernest**, a lifelong bachelor, in 1955.

1914

Cook's becomes the first travel agent to offer pleasure trips by plane. A half-hour ride in a converted Handley-Page bomber costs two guineas.

1919

Thomas Cook & Son changes its status, becoming a limited company.

1924

As **Cook's** continues to increase its dominance of world travel, the company moves to new, more spacious headquarters in Berkeley Street, London.

1926

Charles Lindbergh crosses the Atlantic in the *Spirit of St Louis*.

1927

Frank and **Ernest** end their direct involvement with the family business, selling it to La Compagnie Internationale des Wagons-Lits et des Grands Express Européens, the owner's of the Orient Express, for £3.5 million.

1928

In the depths of the depression, **Cook's** is forced to lay off staff and sell most of its renowned Nile fleet.

1931

War breaks out in Europe and **Cook's** is confiscated as enemy property, afterwards becoming a subsidiary of Britain's mainline railway companies.

1939

In the post-war period the company's fortunes revived under a variety of ownerships, and in 1992 it was acquired by Westdeutsche Landesbank. Today, Thomas Cook remains one of the world's largest travel companies, leading worldwide in businesses ranging from travel agencies and tour operations (including a modern fleet of Nile cruisers) to traveller's cheques and global assistance.

NORTH OF THE BORDER

Thomas Cook's background as a printer meant that the publishing of guidebooks and brochures was a natural extension of his excursion business. By 1894, when this list of Cook's Scottish tours appeared, the company offered customers a choice of over 200 promotional compendiums.

Today, the journey from England to Scotland requires little time or effort. No one would consider a tour of the Highlands and lochs a major undertaking. In contrast, Thomas Cook's ground-breaking first trip to Scotland in 1846 proved to be fraught with difficulties and showed just how great the hurdles were that he had to overcome in developing his excursion business.

To begin with, there was no rail link between the two countries. Cook first of all attempted to get to Edinburgh by steamer from Newcastle, but his negotiations with the steamship companies proved futile. He was therefore forced to take the western route: by train from Leicester to Fleetwood, then to Ardrossan by steamer and finally to Glasgow by rail. About 350 passengers set off with Thomas Cook in the first week of July 1846 on his inaugural Scottish venture, but it proved to be anything but plain sailing. Looking back in 1866 on his first 20 years of Scottish tours, Cook was to admit: 'a miserable night we had in crossing by the Mull of Galloway and the Ayrshire Coast to the port of debarcation [sic]. We had issued too many First Class Tickets for the Cabin accommodation, and that gave rise to some unpleasantness, which was intensified by a wet night'.

Cook's Scottish tours caught the public imagination and in those first 20 years he personally made over 60 trips north of the border and arranged tours for more than 50,000 people. The ultimate success of this enterprise was instrumental in establishing Cook's reputation as an excursion organiser and yet the outcome was never a foregone conclusion. Cook faced two constant threats: one was the capriciousness of the companies on which he depended for transport and the other was that of the general public. In 1863, for example, at short notice, the railway authorities refused to allow any excursions from England, thus effectively wiping out Cook's entire season. The previous year, the International Exhibition in London had dominated public attention, leaving Cook with 'almost a blank year for Scottish Excursions'.

Things did improve. In 1876, the Midland Railway opened the first direct rail link with Scotland (£5 9s 6d for a first-class ticket to Edinburgh from London) and by the time this 1894 brochure was produced, the building of new roads, bridges and railways had completed the opening up of the 'land of the mountain and the flood' to the excursionist.

Among Cook's most popular Scottish destinations were the hills and lochs on the Highlands and Trossachs Tour. Nine-day, fully conducted tours, priced at 12 guineas, left Edinburgh on a Wednesday eight times during the summer season. The brochure laid out the daily itinerary in great detail, including hotel, meal and baggage arrangements. It ended by advising participants that 'to acquire additional interest in this magnificent tour' they should peruse at leisure a reading list that included Scott's *Lady of the Lake* and *Rob Roy*, and Miss Porter's *Scottish Chiefs*.

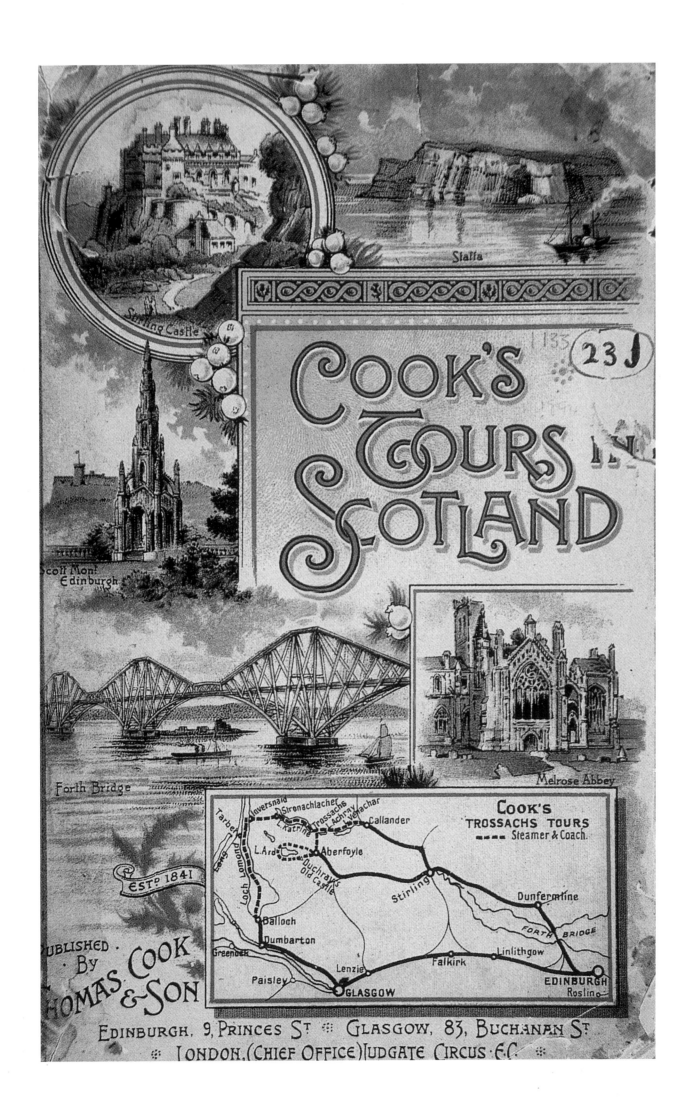

Stirling Castle

Staffa

Scott Mont
Edinburgh

COOK'S
TOURS IN
SCOTLAND

1135

23 J

Melrose Abbey

Forth Bridge

ESTD 1841

COOK'S
TROSSACHS TOURS
Steamer & Coach.

Inversnaid · Stronachlacher · Trossachs · Achray · L.Vennachar · Callander
L.Katrine
Tarbet · L.Ard · Aberfoyle
Loch Lomond · Duchrays · Old Castle · Stirling · Dunfermline
FORTH BRIDGE
Balloch
Dumbarton · Linlithgow
Greenock · Lenzie · Falkirk
Paisley · GLASGOW · EDINBURGH · Roslin

PUBLISHED
· BY
THOMAS COOK
& SON

EDINBURGH, 9, PRINCES ST · GLASGOW, 83, BUCHANAN ST
LONDON, (CHIEF OFFICE) LUDGATE CIRCUS · E.C.

THE EMERALD ISLE

Cook's brochures always presented a dazzling array of specimen tours and travel options and this 1892 guide to the delights of Ireland was no exception.

Cook's first tour of Ireland took place in 1849. Things seemed to be progressing smoothly until, as Cook later wrote, 'one of the leading Railways of England', whose sway over the Irish railway companies was considerable, 'threatened various steps in the event of our proposals being agreed to'. For 17 years from 1855 the Irish railways therefore refused to deal with Cook or accept his tickets.

When Cook was permitted to resume his Irish tours he found that the English railway company, still clearly believing that it had no need of Cook, had announced that it 'would appoint an Agent in opposition to us, and should demand the same arrangements for such Agent as had been accorded to us'. Such copycat tactics were typical of Cook's early experience but, as he righteously declared, 'if certain people have no ideas of their own, we can continue finding plenty for ourselves and them too, leaving the public to appreciate and discriminate'.

Cook not only had to deal with the pettiness of his rivals, he also had to work hard to sell his destinations to the public. The introduction to this 1892 brochure for the independent traveller declares its firm belief that 'a much greater number of tourists would visit the "Emerald Isle" for their annual summer holiday than is at present the case, were they aware of its many and varied attractions'. Any potential visitor was also reassured that 'a holiday in Ireland need not be a very expensive matter; the whole cost of a tour could, we think, be brought within the compass of about Five Pounds per week'.

The brochure offered a bewildering array of 21 possible routes to and through Ireland. For the hapless tourist this proved to be only a small sample of Cook's repertoire: 'the list,

extensive though it is . . . represents but a few specimens of the almost endless varieties of combination that can be arranged by our unique system of Tourist Coupon and Tickets'. Tour number two, at a cost of £7 4s 6d first class, £5 1s second and £4 2s 6d third, was as follows: London, Oxford, Warwick, Chester, Holyhead, Dublin, rail to Dundalk and Warrenpoint, horse-drawn carriage via Rostrevor and the Mourne Mountains to Newcastle, then by rail to Belfast, steamer to Glasgow and finally back to London by rail via Melrose, Carlisle, Leeds, Sheffield and Bedford.

A decision on the route made, independent travellers who wished to see even more of Ireland had the option of availing themselves of one of Cook's many tours from Dublin. Number 27, for example, priced for the three classes of travel at £5 18s 6d, £5 0s 6d and £3 11s 6d, set off for Galway via Athlone and Athenry, then to Clifden and back by carriage, on to the train for Limerick, via Mallow and Killarney, where another carriage made the journey to Bantry with stops at Kenmare and Glengariff, back on to the train with visits to Bandon and Cork, a return carriage ride to Blarney to kiss the famous stone, and then back to Dublin. With such an array of tours available, it was probably easiest to pick a tour number at random.

Finally, Cook's strongly advised independent travellers 'to provide themselves with a supply of Cook's Hotel Coupons, which are issued at a uniform rate of Ten and Sixpence per day, providing for bedroom, light, service, meat breakfast, and dinner at table d'hôte'. The hotels which accepted them, Cook's assured its customers, were 'the best in every city or district'. And holders of these coupons 'may rely on being well received and well treated, and their use obviates the necessity for many a "wordy warfare" over the settlement of hotel bills'.

Tours & Excursions

293

Emerald Isle.

CLIFDEN
Connemara

Rostrevor

Killarney

A. THOM & Cº Lᵀᴰ
DUBLIN.

PUBLISHED BY THOMAS COOK & SON
DUBLIN- 43 DAME ST., BELFAST. 27 ROYAL AVENUE.
LONDON (CHIEF OFFICE) LUDGATE CIRCUS. E.C.

COOK'S EXCURSIONIST

The Excursionist *was first published by Thomas Cook in May 1851 at the time of London's World's Fair. This version of the cover first appeared in 1890; it was printed in colour from June 1897. It shows (top left) a view down Fleet Street in London towards St Paul's Cathedral with a flag flying above Cook's headquarters at Ludgate Circus.*

Joseph Paxton's Crystal Palace, the centrepiece of London's Great Exhibition of 1851, contained an incredible 293,655 panes of glass and was officially opened by Queen Victoria on 1 May 1851. Two days later, on 3 May, a reproduction of this architectural marvel appeared on the masthead of a cheaply produced, 16-page penny weekly: *Cook's Exhibition Herald and Excursion Advertiser*. Its mission statement was: 'to promote the comfort and pleasure of other excursionists, by the indication of the best routes, descriptions of the most interesting objects by the way, and attention to the physical, social and financial circumstances of patrons and companions'.

By the time the Great Exhibition closed on 15 October more than six million people had visited this first World's Fair, 150,000 alone under the aegis of Thomas Cook. The *Herald* had proved a great success in promoting Cook's business and so, while the Crystal Palace was dismantled and the exhibits packed away, Cook renamed his newsletter *Cook's Excursionist and Cheap Trip Advertiser* and continued publication. The masthead now read: 'Edited, Printed and Published, by T. Cook, Excursion Manager, Leicester'.

The *Excursionist,* the one word that remained constant in the title until May 1902, proved an ideal and flexible vehicle for Cook to promote his tourist services. In his typically florid prose he advertised upcoming tours and excursions, regaled

readers with reports of successful trips, railed against his detractors and the deficiencies of the railway companies and even found time to promote the temperance cause. Cook sought to educate his readership about travel, to dispel misunderstandings about his organisation and to provide copious details of the possibilities his tickets and tours offered. Above all, it was a distinctly personal journal.

The size, frequency and design of the periodical varied considerably in the early years, as did its title. Cook soon abandoned the idea of producing a weekly and instead declared his intention to publish 'as and when required'. This initially meant that the *Excursionist* was produced only during the summer tourist season but, as Cook's business grew, it settled down to become a two-penny monthly. The evolution of Cook's business was also reflected in the constant renaming of the publication. When a second International Exhibition was held in London in 1862, it became *Cook's Excursionist and International Exhibition and Bazaar Advertiser;* to herald the firm's first American tour in 1866 it was rechristened *Cook's Excursionist and European and American Tourist Advertiser*. Only in 1870, by which time John Mason Cook had taken over the editorial reins, did it become known as *Cook's Excursionist and Home and Foreign Tourist Advertiser*, a title it retained until May 1902. In that month the *Excursionist* was replaced by *The Traveller's Gazette*, which continued to be published until 1939.

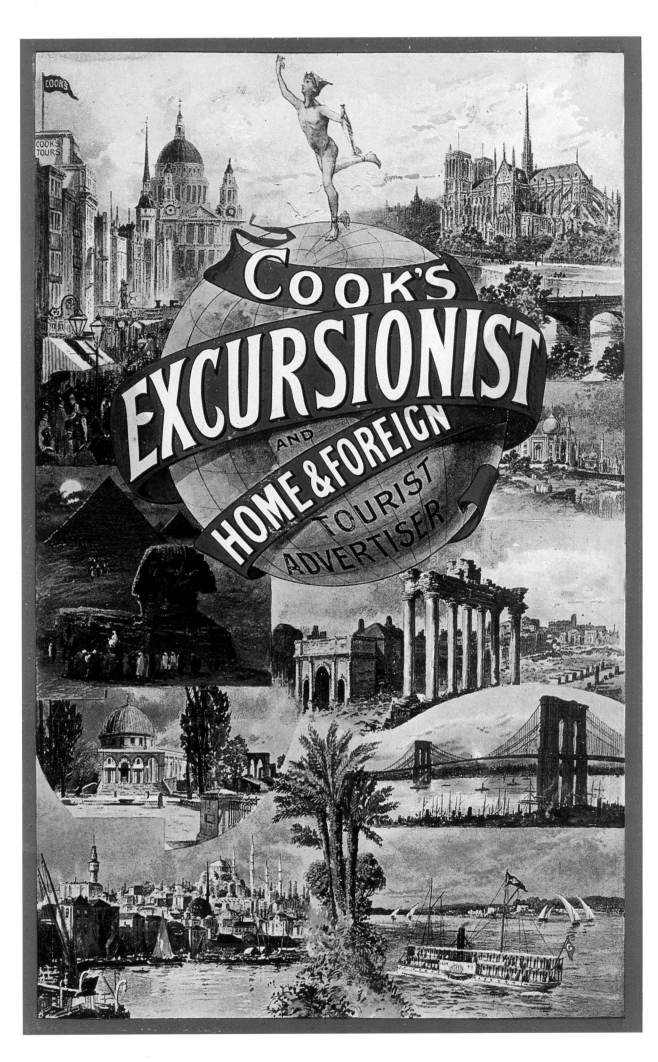

ALWAYS READ THE SMALL PRINT

This advertisement for Merryweather's patent 'kit-bag' fire escape first appeared in the pages of Cook's Excursionist *is 1899. The fire escape, priced at £3, had been supplied to the Khedive of Egypt and it was declared that, 'No visitor to Hotels should be without one of these simple Life-saving Appliances'.* (Coloured)

In the first issue of the *Excursionist* newspaper in May 1851, Thomas Cook announced his intention to 'fill one half of each Number with Advertisements of Excursion arrangements, accommodation, books of travel, maps and other commercial matters relating to the objects which come within the scope of our arrangements and design'. The prices were initially set 'on a scale of unprecedented liberality': railway or steamboat-excursion advertisements cost 5s for up to half a column; accommodation notices were charged a 'nominal' 1s per six lines (plus 1s 6d duty) and 2d for each additional line; and 'Other advertisements of a respectable character shall be inserted on most reasonable terms'. Cook made only one proviso: 'As Excursionists generally want very little physic, we have no desire for medicinal rostrums at any price'.

Hotels, and temperance hotels in particular, dominated the back pages of early editions of the magazine. Alongside notices for Cook's own temperance boarding house in Leicester were simple messages advising readers of the attractive accommodation available at a range of resting places, including Smithard's Temperance Hotel in Derby, Farish's property in Chester and Aitken's temperance establishment in Glasgow.

Increasingly, as the *Excursionist* grew in popularity, hotel notices were joined by elaborately designed advertisements for an assortment of associated travel paraphernalia. Among the first was Knox, Samuel, Dickson, purveyors of 'cheap souvenirs of Scotland', and James S Carter, boot maker and tourists' outfitter. From his premises at 295 Oxford Street, London, Carter offered customers an array of travel goods that included alpine boots,

portable baths, felt hats, wine bags and gossamer veils.

By the 1870s the floodgates had opened and Cook's original dictum was swept away: patent remedies joined outfitters, luggage suppliers and a host of exotic travel accessories. White's, for instance, announced that over 500 medical men declared their Moc-main Lever Truss to be 'the most effective treatment of HERNIA'; Oleridge's Balm of Columbia was advertised as 'the best and only certain remedy for preserving, strengthening, beautifying, or restoring the hair, whiskers or moustaches'; and Eno's ran a series of sermon-like ads for their Fruit Salt, an elixir whose universal powers to cure and revitalise were available to anyone 'whose duties require them to undergo Mental or Unnatural Excitement or Strain'.

The value of the *Excursionist* to advertisers was summed up in a notice in the American edition: 'COOK'S EXCURSIONIST has a large and increasing circulation among a class that advertisers are particularly desirous of reaching. It is freely circulated on board the chief Atlantic and other steamers, at the principal hotels, and through its list of subscribers and the various offices of the firm, reaches and is read by a large percentage of the public travelling for pleasure'.

The back pages of Cook's magazine became a delightful testament to the inventiveness of the Victorian mind. Here the ardent traveller could fulfil every foreseeable need with a host of ingenious, if sometimes dubious, travel aids including: the Ashantee pocket hammock, Keating's Persian insect destroying powder, Roach's sea-sickness draughts, J Allen's portable Turkish bath, Wilmot's patent tablet label, and the unattributed magic umbrella.

"KIT BAG ESCAPE.

COOK'S CONDUCTED TOURS

Like the guardian angel in this 1901 illustration, Cook's tour guides took care of their charges from the moment of departure, smoothing the way around the pitfalls of foreign travel.
(Coloured)

When the train carrying Thomas Cook's first excursionists pulled out of Leicester station on Monday, 5 July 1841, Cook was among their number. He travelled with the party the 11 miles to Loughborough and was on hand throughout the day to ensure that everything ran smoothly. Cook was again on hand when he led his first party to Liverpool and North Wales in 1845, again when he ventured to the Highlands of Scotland the following year and again on his firm's first European tour in 1855.

This 'conducting' of tours was initially determined by necessity. With little in the way of a tourist infrastructure and no system in existence to make advance bookings, Cook had to be on hand to ensure that everything ran smoothly, to find and pay for hotel accommodation and to hire transport to local sites.

Cook established many lasting friendships through this personal contact with his customers and his early tours had the atmosphere of a family outing rather than a commercial undertaking. Apart from necessity, the conducting of tours proved to have additional benefits. Matilda Lincolne, who with her sisters accompanied Cook on his 1855 tour to Antwerp, Brussels, Cologne, Frankfurt, Heidelberg, Baden-Baden, Strasbourg and Paris, noted: 'Many of our friends thought us too independent and adventurous to leave the shores of old England, and thus plunge into foreign lands not beneath Victoria's sway, with no protecting relative, but we can only say that we hope this will not be our last Excursion of the kind. We would venture anywhere with such a guide and guardian as Mr. Cook, for there was not one of his party but felt perfectly safe when under his care'.

In the early years, conducted tours were organised on an irregular basis. Plans for proposed trips were announced in the

TRAVEL IN COMFORT !

SELECT ..
CONDUCTED
.. TOURS

SUMMER SEASON. 1908.

CONDUCTOR-TRAVEL-HOTEL-DRIVES-&c.

FRANCE
BELGIUM
SWITZERLAND
GERMANY & AUSTRIA
NORWAY, DENMARK, and SWEDEN
HOLLAND
THE RHINE
THE DOLOMITES
THE SALZKAMMERGUT
LUTHER'S LAND
SCOTLAND, IRELAND
ENGLISH LAKES
&c., &c.

ILLUSTRATED BOOKLETS AND SEASON'S SYNOPSIS FREE.

THOS. COOK & SON.

pages of the *Excursionist* in order 'to elicit the desires of intending travellers'. At this stage the exact dates and details of the trip often remained undecided. When Cook first announced his intention to undertake a tour round the world he declared: 'The question most difficult to decide is, which route to take from San Francisco to India. The China route is the most expeditious, but we incline to the idea that most English Travellers would prefer to get glimpses of our own Colonies of New Zealand and Australia'. In the end the northern route won out.

The size of the travelling party was also fluid. It was common not only for people to join a tour along its route, but also to leave it, perhaps temporarily, to travel under their own steam. The attempts to muster sufficient support from the public to make a tour financially viable were not always successful. In August 1866 the *Excursionist* regretted: 'the number of those who have intimated a desire to accompany Mr. Cook to America in the month of September, is not sufficient to justify the carrying out of the proposal, and it is therefore abandoned'.

In the wake of Cook's pioneering tours it became impossible and also unnecessary to accompany every tourist on their journey. Improvements in travel services, and Cook's agency to sell tickets for the major rail and steamship companies, made independent travel increasingly the norm. But Cook was continually irked to find that 'A great many people. . . cannot divest themselves of the idea that in order to avail themselves of the low rates charged for our tickets, they must join a party'. The conducted tour remained a distinctive, if proportionately small, part of Cook's business but, as the American *Excursionist* pointed out in the 1880s: 'ninety per cent. of our clientage [are] independent travelers, who purchase their tickets from us to use at their pleasure, making breaks of journey where and when they will'.

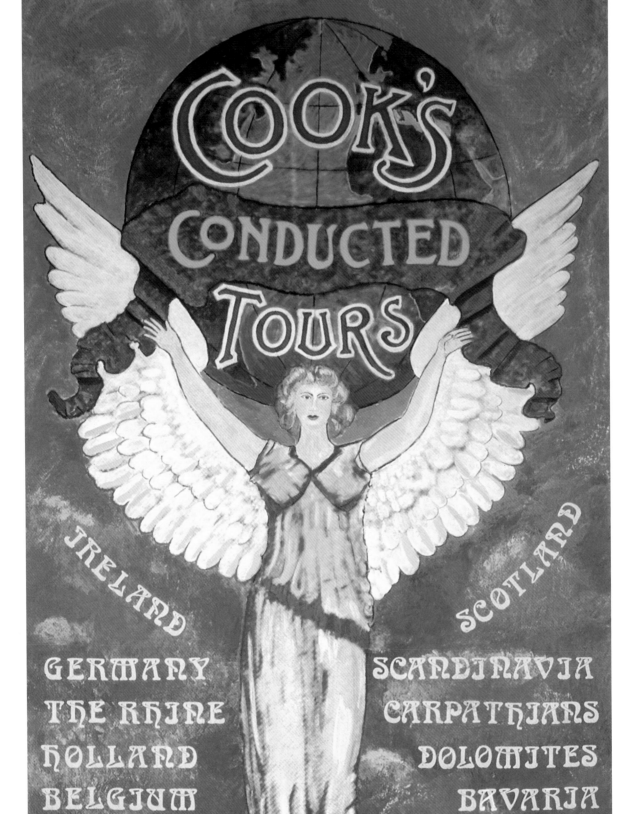

COOK'S CONDUCTED TOURS

IRELAND

GERMANY
THE RHINE
HOLLAND
BELGIUM
AUSTRIA

SCOTLAND

SCANDINAVIA
CARPATHIANS
DOLOMITES
BAVARIA
ARDENNES

COOK'S POPULAR TOURS

This 1905 illustration portrays some of the destinations which, thanks to Thomas Cook & Son, had become 'as much the winter playgrounds of the middle-class traveller as of the millionaire'. (Coloured)

For the socially conscious Victorians, class was everything. The Establishment therefore felt obliged to protest when Cook's system of cheap tours brought the prospect of foreign travel within the reach of a class of people that had previously never left Britain's shores. Cook was pilloried in journals and magazines, his tours satirised as 'Cook's Circus' and complaints levelled at the hordes he unleashed upon the Continent. One particularly vitriolic attack came from Charles Lever, British vice-consul in La Spezia, who accused Cook of swamping Europe with 'everything that is low-bred, vulgar, and ridiculous'.

The *Telegraph* newspaper reported in 1873: 'It is, or has been, the fashion amongst some empty-headed persons to sneer at "Cook's Tourists". Pretending to imagine that the pleasures of travel should be reserved for the upper classes, they protested against the beauties of Nature being examined by any but persons of high quality, and seemed to think that the grey Highlands, the quaint Belgian cities, the castled Rhine crags, the glaciers, mountains, and waterfalls of Switzerland, and the blue plains of Italy, were exhibitions which should be open only to holders of high-priced stall tickets'. The fact that Cook was soon making travel arrangements for many of the same people who had once been so critical, 'amongst them Dukes, Archbishops, and members of every class of respectable society', meant that he could 'well afford to disregard either spoken scoff or printed satire'.

Cook's continued to cater to both ends of the travel market. For the wealthy who wished to be pampered and cared for every step of the way there were Cook's Select Conducted Tours; for those of more moderate means, happy to travel under less luxurious conditions, Cook's developed a programme of Popular Tours. This system, 'while leaving the traveller at perfect liberty as to his movements, includes both travel and hotel expenses in one fixed charge'. For the former group, where status was everything, prices were invariably quoted in the aristocratic guinea; Popular Tour costs usually appeared in pounds, shillings and pence and unashamedly offered 'exceedingly low prices'.

The £10 10s (i.e., 10 guineas) tours on this illustration include Cook's 'famous Tour to Rome'. The fare included 'Second Class Travel Ticket to Rome and back, together with Seven Days' Hotel Accommodation, viz., Five Days at Rome, One Day at Genoa on the outward journey, and One Day at Turin on returning. The accommodation consists of breakfast, luncheon, and dinner, bedroom, lights, and service'. Holders of these tickets were also accorded the 'privilege' of accompanying the conducted tour on the journey to Rome free of charge.

Other £10 10s tours offered similar provisions for visiting the South of France or Switzerland and, in all cases, ticket holders had the option of prolonging their stay for up to 25 days. For those wishing to spend less, a week in Normandy was on offer for £4 17s 6d, a week in Holland and Belgium for £5 5s and a fortnight in the Channel Islands for £5 10s 6d.

Cook's £10-10 Tours

To Rome

to the South of France

and to Switzerland

The Forum.

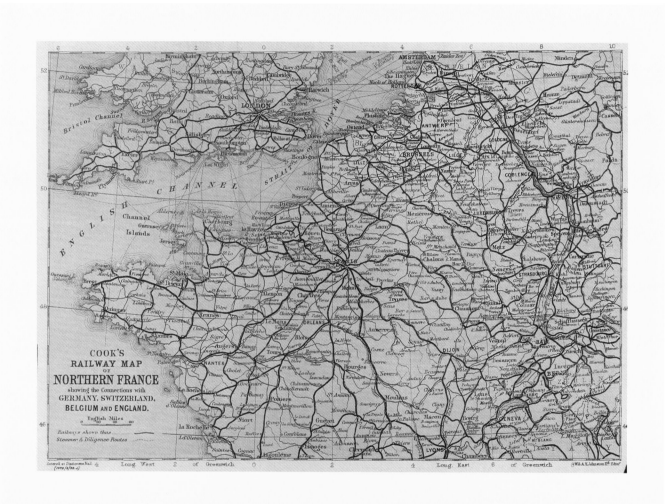

COOK'S
RAILWAY MAP
OF
NORTHERN FRANCE
showing the Connections with
GERMANY, SWITZERLAND,
BELGIUM AND ENGLAND.

English Miles
0   20   40   60

Railways shown thus
Steamer & Diligence Routes

INTO THE HEART OF EUROPE

A romantic view of journey's end adorns the brochure cover overleaf advertising Cook's programme of conducted tours to the Rhine and Switzerland for the 1891 season. (Coloured)

Chance played an important role in the expansion of Thomas Cook's tourist business. Many of his important new ventures were the result of unheralded happenings. For example, it was a chance meeting with Joseph Paxton, architect of the Crystal Palace, and John Ellis of the Midland Railway that led to Cook's successful association with the Great Exhibition of 1851.

By 1863, although he had made brief forays across the English Channel, for instance, at the time of Paris's International Exhibition in 1855, Cook was concentrating his energies on the extension of his system of Scottish tours. The decision of the railway companies not to allow any excursions from England that year scuppered his plans. Cook's resourcefulness was put to the test and he responded by introducing his first season of combined tours to Paris and Switzerland.

Over 2000 tourists travelled to Paris under Cook's arrangements that year, at a cost of 17s 6d, with a supplement of 10s for first class. A quarter of these continued on to Switzerland, where most joined one of Cook's three personally conducted tours. The last of these left on 15 September, and among the 'interesting incidents' was 'the accidental falling in with a Florentine Countess, accompanied by two lovely children, and a courteous invitation from her ladyship to visit the Palace of a Minister of State in Florence, whenever we may extend these beyond the Alps, which we hope will be in . . . 1864'.

Cook's Swiss tours expanded rapidly, again sometimes helped by unforeseen circumstances. In 1866, there was a significant rise in Cook's numbers as, 'in consequence of the war

[between Prussia/Italy and Austria], there is a concentration on free and peaceful Switzerland, whilst Italy and the Rhine districts are nearly closed against Tourists'.

In 1892, Thomas Cook & Son's programme of tours covered the entire continent of Europe, and beyond, but Switzerland remained a perennial favourite. The *Excursionist* printed a full list of dates for the forthcoming season. There were departures for Paris every Monday and Saturday, and the popular Paris and Switzerland conducted tour ran six times between May and September. The Rhine and Switzerland tours featured in this brochure also took place half a dozen times a season, leaving London on Mondays.

Two different routes were available: the first, which took 30 days, visited Belgium, the Rhine, the Black Forest, Switzerland and Paris and cost £42 10s for first class, £38 15s in second. A shorter 18-day tour also took members to Antwerp, Brussels, Cologne, down the Rhine by steamer and around the principal sites of Switzerland, but skipped the Black Forest. The fare was £29 10s first class, £25 15s second class. Cook's brochure provided exact details of the schedule to be followed, including the mileage covered each day and a list of the hotels where the party would be stopping, such as the Hotel Holland (Baden-Baden), Hotel du Cygne (Lucerne), Hotel de l'Ours (Grindelwald) and Hotel Beau-Rivage (Ouchy). A decade later, a virtually identical tour was still on offer to Cook's clients. The first route was now covered in 25 days and the fare had been reduced to £39 15s and £36 5s in first and second class respectively; the second route, still 18 days, cost £30 10s and £27 10s.

THE RHINE & SWITZERLAND 1891

Cook's

Conducted Tours.

W.C. Kerr

THOMAS COOK AND THE NEW WORLD

When the Great East River Suspension Bridge linking Brooklyn and Manhattan opened in May 1883, it was hailed as the eighth wonder of the world. Its 1595-feet span, by far the largest in the world at that time, made a suitable backdrop for the cover of this 1891 booklet of Cook's American tours. (Coloured)

On 29 November 1865, Thomas Cook left Liverpool aboard the *City of Boston* on his first, trail-blazing voyage to the United States. What he described as 'the black cloud of the American [civil] war' had only just lifted, but he was still able to travel 'over about 4000 miles of American and Canadian Railroads, submitting to the managers of lines our proposals for Special Excursions and Circular Tours'.

Cook declared this trip 'the greatest journey ever made in our travelling life [so far]'. He returned to England having successfully negotiated concessionary first-class return fares across the Atlantic (21 guineas from Glasgow, 25 guineas from Liverpool) and having decided upon a 'uniform rate of two cents (one penny) per mile' on the railways. He also laid the foundations for the company's first organised tour to America, personally conducted by his son, John Mason Cook, which left England the following May.

Despite what John Mason described as the great difficulty of leading 'an Excursion Party over nearly 4000 miles of a country never before visited by the "Conductor"', he came away favourably impressed: 'my views have been altered very much, both as regards America and the Americans'. He held 'personal interviews with at least a hundred Railway and Steamboat Officials' and left the country reassured that 'the 41 Series of Tickets that we had arranged were *all* recognised and in working order'.

Further escorted tours followed with whirlwind itineraries that would exhaust the modern traveller. Tourists in May 1874 paid an all-inclusive fare of £80 that included return passage to America and 40 days of travel under the direct supervision of Mr W A Short. As well as visits to Niagara Falls, the battlefields of the Civil War and the Capitol in Washington, members of the party met with President Grant and visited the New Masonic Hall in Philadelphia, the lunatic asylums of New York and the large flooring mills in Richmond.

Despite these early successes, Thomas Cook found his efforts to expand further in the US hindered by the 'Discord of Railway Companies and jealousies of agents employed to sell Tickets'. A brief and acrimonious partnership with E M Jenkins of Philadelphia further hindered progress, but by 1891 the company was proud to announce 'that there is no tourist resort on this great Continent for which we cannot furnish information and tickets'. As proof, Cook's was able to offer the independent traveller a round-trip railway ticket from New York, valid for nine months, that took the tourist to Chicago, Kansas City, Williams (for the Grand Canyon), Los Angeles, San Francisco, Ogden, Salt Lake City, Colorado Springs, Denver, St Louis and finally back to New York (with optional stopovers at no extra charge at Niagara Falls, Philadelphia, Baltimore and Washington). The cost: $148.20.

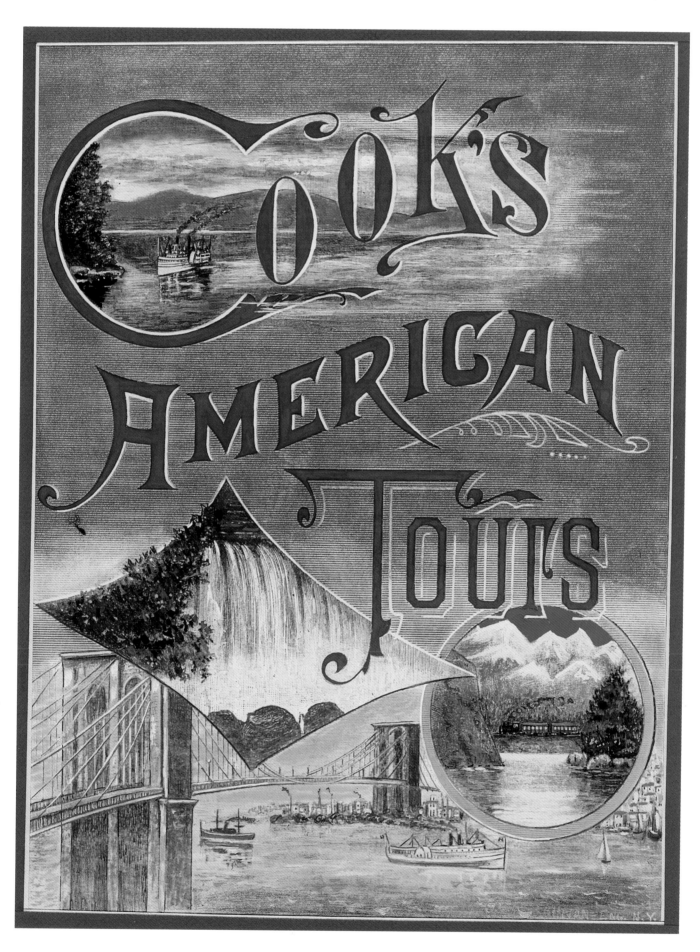

EASTER TOUR TO BELGIUM.

COOK'S SPECIAL TOUR
TO
ANTWERP AND BRUSSELS,

Visiting ANTWERP, BRUSSELS, THE BATTLEFIELD
OF WATERLOO, &c.,

Leaving LONDON, Thursday, April 11th, 1895.

INCLUSIVE FARE:—

SECOND CLASS THROUGHOUT - - **£5 5s. 0d.**

ITINERARY.

THURSDAY, APRIL 11TH.—The Conductor will leave Liverpool Street Station, Great Eastern Railway, at 8·30 p.m. for Harwich, and thence by one of the magnificent steamers of the Great Eastern Railway Company for Antwerp. Passengers from the Midland counties and North of England can join at Harwich, the tickets being available to commence the journey at March, or any other Great Eastern station, at the same fare as from London. Members of the party wishing to travel first class on the steamer between Harwich and Antwerp in both directions will be charged 11s. extra. Notice of this must be given when paying deposit.

FRIDAY, APRIL 12TH.—Arrive at Antwerp about 10·0 a.m., where the remainder of the day will be spent, a carriage drive being provided.

SATURDAY, APRIL 13TH.—Leave by morning train for Brussels, where the remainder of the day will be spent. Brussels is well provided with Theatres, Concert Halls, &c., and military bands play frequently in the parks and public gardens. (*Cook's Tourist Office, 41, Rue de la Madeleine.*)

SUNDAY, APRIL 14TH.—To be spent in Brussels.

MONDAY, APRIL 15TH.—A carriage excursion will be made to the Battlefield of Waterloo, to visit the site of the celebrated battle of June 18th, 1815.

TUESDAY, APRIL 16TH.—An interesting carriage drive will be arranged for visiting the principal public buildings and sights. The party will leave by express train for Antwerp, and embark by steamer for Harwich.

WEDNESDAY, APRIL 17TH.—Arrive at Harwich and proceed by train to London, due at 8·5 a.m.

Excursion or Ordinary Tickets are issued from the principal provincial towns to London and back in connection with the above tour; full particulars can be obtained from any of Cook's Tourist Offices.

Deposits received and names registered at any of the Offices of

THOS. COOK & SON,
CHIEF OFFICE—Ludgate Circus, London, E.C.

EASTER HOLIDAY TOUR TO HOLLAND.

COOK'S CONDUCTED TOUR
TO
HOLLAND,

Visiting ROTTERDAM, THE HAGUE, SCHEVENINGEN, AMSTERDAM,
ZAANDAM, ALKMAAR, &c.

Leaving LONDON, Thursday, April 11th, 1895.

INCLUSIVE FARE—

SECOND CLASS THROUGHOUT ... **£5 15s. 0d.**

Saloon on Steamer in both directions, 11s. additional.

ITINERARY.

THURSDAY, APRIL 11TH.—The Conductor will leave Liverpool Street Station, Great Eastern Railway, at 8·30 p.m. for Harwich, and thence by one of the magnificent steamers of the Great Eastern Railway Company for Rotterdam. Passengers from the Midland counties and North of England can join at Harwich, the tickets being available to commence the journey at March, at the same fare as from London. Members of the party wishing to travel first class on the steamer in both directions can do so at an additional charge of 11s. Notice of this must be given when paying deposit, in order that the necessary berths can be secured.

GOOD FRIDAY, APRIL 12TH.—The steamer will call at the new port, Hook of Holland, and proceed to Rotterdam (*Hotel Weimar*).

SATURDAY, APRIL 13TH.—Leave Rotterdam by morning train for the Hague (*Hotel du Vieux Doelen*), passing *en route* Schiedam, celebrated for its distilleries and windmills, and Delft, a town that once headed the pottery trade with its Delftware. During the stay a visit will be made to Scheveningen.

EASTER SUNDAY, APRIL 14TH.—To be spent at the Hague. For this day no programme or excursion is planned, members being free to make their own arrangements. Many of the Museums and Picture Galleries are open, and bands play in the beautiful Park during the afternoon.

EASTER MONDAY, APRIL 15TH.—Travel by morning train from the Hague to Amsterdam (*Hotel Pays-Bas*), where the day will be spent.

TUESDAY, APRIL 16TH.—Excursion by steamer to Zaandam and Alkmaar. Return to Amsterdam in time for dinner, and leave by train at 8·30 p.m. for the Hook of Holland, and embark on the Great Eastern Company's steamer for Harwich.

WEDNESDAY, APRIL 17TH.—Arrive at Harwich, and proceed by train to London, due at 8·5 a.m.

Deposits received and names registered at any of the Offices of

THOS. COOK & SON,
CHIEF OFFICE—Ludgate Circus, London, E.C.

EASTER IN ROME.

COOK'S CHEAP CONDUCTED
TOUR TO ROME,

Leaving London, Thursday, April 11th, 1895.

INCLUSIVE FARE - - - **£13 13 0**

The Conductor will leave London Bridge Station at 9·0 a.m. on Thursday, April 11th, *en route* for Paris, via Newhaven and Dieppe. Spend Friday morning in Paris and leave by 2·45 p.m. train from the Lyons Station for Turin and Rome.

Arrive Rome 6·35 a.m., Sunday, April 14th. Five days in Easter Week will be spent in Rome, the capital of the Kingdom of Italy, and the seat of the Popes. A visit to Rome is the grandest experience of a European tour, and members of this party during their five days' stay in the city will have ample opportunity for visiting the principal classic ruins, St. Peter's and other churches, the Vatican, the largest palace in the world, the Royal and other palaces, the many villas full of art treasures, and for making interesting excursions.

The party will leave Rome by train at 8·50 p.m. on Thursday, April 18th, arriving in London at 7·50 a.m. on Sunday, April 21st.

COOK'S CHEAP RETURN TICKETS
BETWEEN
LONDON AND ROME,

(Via Paris and Modane),

Available to start between March 31st and April 11th. Available for 30 Days.

FARES:

	Via CALAIS.	Via DIEPPE.
First Class - - - - - -	£14 13s. 0d.	£13 2s. 3d.
Second Class - - - - -	£10 12s. 6d.	£9 6s. 3d.
Third Class to Paris, Second beyond	£9 6s. 0d. - -	£8 17s. 3d.

* By Night Mail Service between London and Paris.

These Tickets are accepted by all trains, express and rapide, except the 8·40 a.m. Turin to Rome and the 8·10 a.m. Rome to Turin.

Passengers holding First Class Tickets can occupy coupé-lits, fauteuils, lits salons, or sleeping cars, on payment of the usual supplement.

Supplement for berth in Sleeping Car Paris-Rome - - - **£2 0s. 2d.**

The Tickets are strictly non-transferable. 56 lbs. of baggage free as far as Modane. In Italy all registered luggage is charged for. Passengers must see their luggage examined by the Customs at the frontiers.

The following is the quickest through service to and from Rome.

Leave London (Victoria) 11·0 a.m., arr. Paris (Nord) 7·0 p.m.; dep. Paris (Lyons) 9·0 p.m., arr. Turin 2·20 p.m.; dep. Turin 2·45 p.m., arr. Genoa 6·14 p.m., Pisa 10·58 p.m., Rome 6·34 a.m. Leave Rome 10·17 p.m., Pisa 4·47 a.m., Genoa 3·46 a.m., arr. Turin 12·30 p.m.; dep. Turin 2·20 p.m., arr. Paris (Lyons) 8·45 a.m.; dep. Paris (Nord) 8·0 a.m., arr. London (Victoria) 4·30 p.m.

EXTENSION TICKETS FOR NAPLES may be obtained in Rome at 33s. 7d. First Class, 23s. 7d. Second Class; or including the ascent of Vesuvius, 53s. 7d. First Class, 43s. 7d. Second Class; or including Naples, Vesuvius, and Pompeii, 56s. 1d. First Class, 45s. 5d. Second Class.

No allowance can be made if the journey is not completed within the time advertised.

HOLY WEEK & EASTER IN SEVILLE,
APRIL 8th to 13th, 1895.
RELIGIOUS CEREMONIES AND PROCESSIONS.
FAIR AT SEVILLE, APRIL 18th to 22nd.

COOK'S RETURN TICKETS TO SEVILLE,

Allowing breaks of journey at PARIS, BORDEAUX, BAYONNE, SAN SEBASTIAN, BURGOS, ESCURIAL, MADRID, ARANJUEZ, CASTILLEJO (for TOLEDO), and CORDOVA.

Available to start between MARCH 29TH and APRIL 15TH, and return any day up to MAY 5TH inclusive (but not more than 30 days in all).

FARES:

	Via CALAIS.	Via DIEPPE.
1st class throughout - - - - -	£14 9 1	£12 18 4
2nd cl. to Paris and back, 1st cl. beyond	£13 8 7	£12 2 4

Passengers can travel by the train de luxe to Madrid on payment of the usual supplement.

CHEAP RETURN TICKETS TO MADRID

Will also be issued, available for 20 days, to start between April 3rd and 13th.

FARES:

	Via CALAIS.	Via DIEPPE.
1st class throughout - - - - -	£12 9 1	£10 18 4
2nd cl. to Paris and back, 1st cl. beyond -	£11 8 7	£10 2 4

These Tickets are available by all Trains except the Sud Express, to travel by which an extra charge of £3 10s. 3d. is made, providing for a sleeping berth between Paris and Madrid.

The above Travelling Tickets, with or without Hotel Coupons, can be obtained at any of the Offices of

THOS. COOK & SON,
Chief Office—Ludgate Circus, London.

For full particulars of the above Tours, see separate Special Programmes, to be obtained free at any of the Offices of
Thos. Cook & Son.

A BED
FOR THE
NIGHT

*This idiosyncratic view of the world
and its inhabitants by Kennedy North,
overleaf, was presented to the travelling
public 'for their joy and instruction' by
Messrs Thomas Cook & Son in 1924.
By the 1920s, Cook's travel arrangements
spanned the globe and its hotel coupons
were accepted on every continent.*

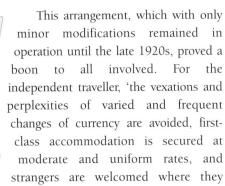

Cook quickly realised on his escorted tours that obtaining accommodation at journey's end was just as fraught with difficulty as the journey itself. Initially, Cook was on hand to secure rooms, to negotiate favourable rates with the proprietor and to pay the group's bill but, as the business grew and he ventured further afield, the inherent limitations of this ad hoc system became increasingly apparent.

Unwary travellers were frequently fleeced by unscrupulous hotelkeepers, who padded out their bills with a host of 'extras'. Consequently, in 1863, Cook persuaded individual hotelkeepers on the Continent to provide a room, lights, service and two main meals for a price 'not exceeding eleven francs a day' to anyone who presented one of Cook's ticket cases. But Thomas Cook still had no means of ensuring that hoteliers stuck to his terms and, with the number of independent travellers growing, he resolved to 'make Hotel prices absolute, and accept money for accommodation in advance'.

In 1868, Cook revolutionised the travel industry when he introduced the first series of Cook's Hotel Coupons priced at eight shillings. These had three detachable sections. The first ensured a room, inclusive of lights and service; the second section secured the holder a breakfast or afternoon tea consisting of tea or coffee, bread and butter, and meat or eggs; and the third could be exchanged for dinner at the table d'hôte.

This arrangement, which with only minor modifications remained in operation until the late 1920s, proved a boon to all involved. For the independent traveller, 'the vexations and perplexities of varied and frequent changes of currency are avoided, first-class accommodation is secured at moderate and uniform rates, and strangers are welcomed where they would otherwise be unknown'. Cook, which only sold coupons in conjunction with the purchase of tickets, benefited from the positive cash flow and the hotel owners from the increase in business.

Thomas Cook admitted with glee that his coupon system, of which he claimed 'sole parentage', had exceeded his 'most sanguine expectations'. By 1871, there were 130 appointed Continental hotels in Cook's system, and annually the company sold more than 50,000 nights' accommodation. Three years later this had risen to nearly 300 hotels worldwide and approximately half a million nights' stay. The properties ranged from the Grand Hotel in Yokohama, the Great Eastern Hotel in Calcutta and the Sherman House in Chicago, to Shepheard's Hotel in Cairo, the Hotel du Lac in Geneva and Cook's Temperance Hotel in Leicester, England.

Cook's coupons were used by great and small alike, as one hotelier found out to his cost. When he was advised that King Leopold II of the Belgians would be calling in for dinner, the table d'hôte was loaded with every conceivable delicacy. The king ate a gargantuan meal and when the bill was presented he insisted on paying with one of Cook's table d'hôte meal coupons.

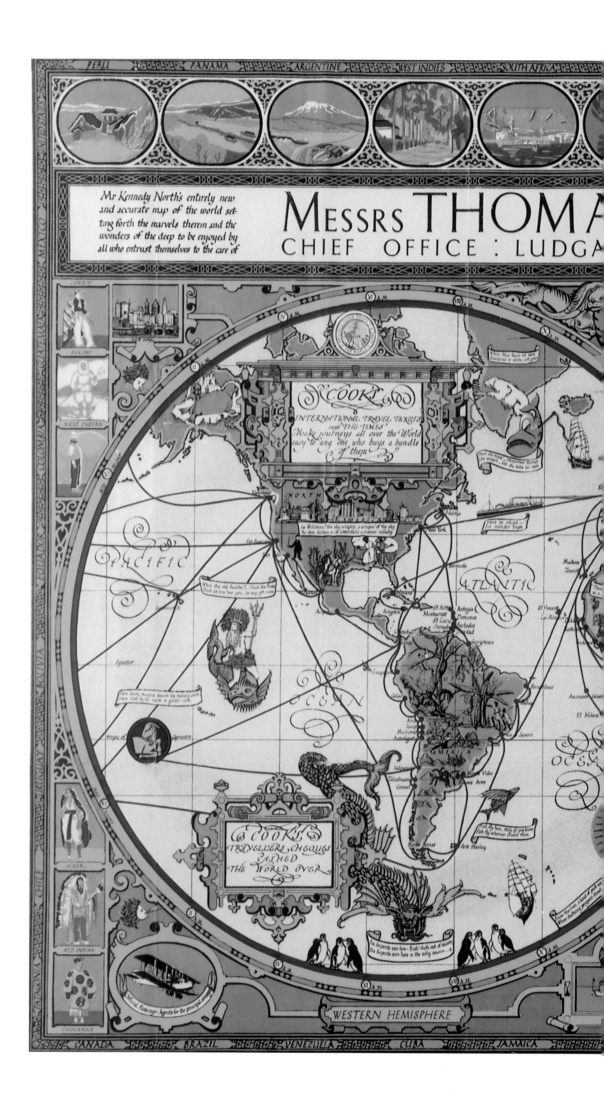

KING OF EGYPT

The brochure cover for Cook's 1904–05 winter season in Egypt. Cook's declared that 'Cairo is not Egypt, but that Egypt is the Nile'; its fleet of Nile craft provided access to the exotic sights that lined the river.

On the morning of 17 November 1869, an orderly procession of some 70 ships of varying size and magnificence formed up behind the French Imperial yacht *Aigle* and slowly made its way through the narrow opening to the Suez Canal. The invited guests on this historic occasion, the official opening of De Lesseps' great engineering feat, included Empress Eugénie of France, the Austrian Emperor, the Crown Prince of Prussia and one Thomas Cook of Leicester, England.

Cook's long and profitable association with the land of the pharaohs had begun in January that same year. He arrived in Egypt at the head of a party of around 30 curious sightseers and chartered two boats to take them up the Nile. The boats, which frequently broke down, were dirty and infested with fleas; the entire crew were constantly demanding baksheesh; and, on their return to Cairo, the group had to remain on board as there was no accommodation available in the capital. On top of all this, Thomas Cook, while bathing in the Nile one Sunday, was swept away by the river and nearly drowned.

The shortcomings experienced on this trip, while irritating, showed Cook the unrivalled opportunity that existed for him in Egypt. The difficulties of travel in this region meant that the country was ideally suited to his brand of tourism, where personal guidance and careful cosseting insulated travellers from the impositions of a foreign culture.

Within a decade of his arrival in Egypt, Cook, ably assisted by his son, had established his supremacy. The consequences of this were immense. Up to that point, Cook's travel business had been largely confined to a lengthy summer season. Egypt, the perfect winter resort, changed Thomas Cook & Son from a European-focused, seasonal operation into a truly international, year-round concern. Egypt also proved to be extremely profitable: by 1888, 10 per cent of the firm's £20,000 profit came from its Egyptian business.

The business-minded John Mason Cook, more concerned with the financial potential that Egypt offered than his father, worked particularly hard to establish the company's hegemony. He was almost single-handedly responsible for the development and operation of Cook's Nile fleet, and his influence over every aspect of Nile travel earned him the sobriquet among locals, 'King of Egypt'. Stories of his all-pervading presence became legend: 'when "the Governor" is pleased to travel up and down his Nile, you may see the natives coming up to him in long lines, salaaming and kissing his hand. When he appears they assemble and chant a song with refrain, "Goood-mees-ta-Cook" '. It is reported that he took Lord Cromer, the most senior British official in Egypt, up the Nile and near Luxor they visited a desert sheikh. The old man 'had no idea that the British had been possessing Egypt all these years; barely knew that the late Khedive was dead'. Amazed, Cromer asked him, 'Haven't you ever heard of me?' The sheikh never had. What about Mr Cook? 'Oh, yes; Cook Pasha; everybody knows Cook Pasha'.

A less charitable comment, which nonetheless illustrated Cook's unrivalled position, was made by a compatriot who declared that Egypt now had four seasons: 'first, flies; second, mosquitoes; third, flying bugs; fourth, Cook's tourists'. This type of disparagement had plagued Cook's business from its earliest days and John Mason, who wintered in his 'kingdom' every year after 1885, set about cultivating a wealthier, more aristocratic clientele. This 1905 brochure, as proof of his success, included an extensive list of the 'Royal and Distinguished Persons who have travelled under the arrangements of Thos. Cook & Son'. The names included the Prince of Wales, the Tsar and Tsarina of Russia, the Emperors and Empresses of Germany and Brazil, the Shah of Persia and the King of Italy.

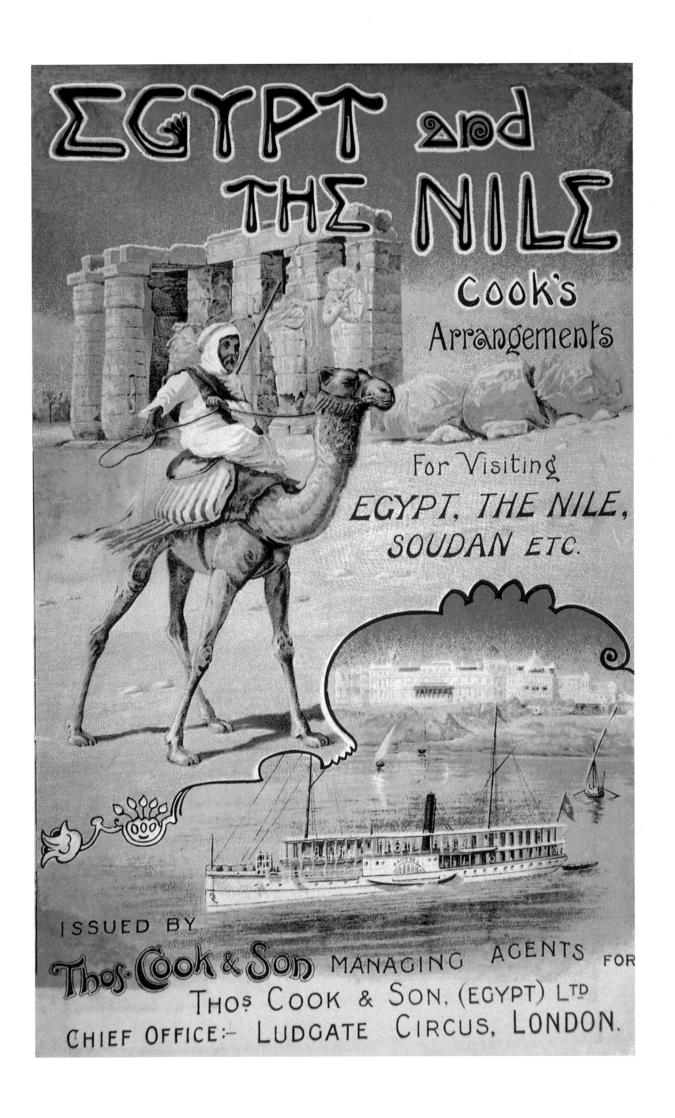

THE LAND OF THE PHARAOHS

Tourists visiting the Middle East frequently combined a visit to Egypt with a stay in Palestine. Egypt, however, is the focus of this 1903 illustration. It shows one of Cook's tourist steamers on the Nile at Aswan. Cook's resplendent Cataract Hotel, which remains in operation to this day, is in the background. (Coloured)

'The Hebrews of the Exodus under the conductorship of Moses on their long and weary march to the Promised Land', declared Cook's *Traveller's Gazette* in October 1908, 'never hungered more ardently for the fleshpots of Egypt than do Gentile and Jew alike for the sunshine and brilliancy of that fascinating land as soon as the month of fog and gloom has arrived. And no wonder, for the climate in Egypt from November to May is the most ideal of all the winter resorts in the world'.

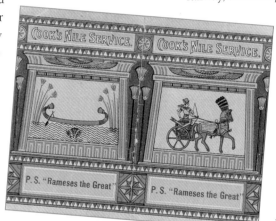

Egypt's warm, dry winter climate was conducive to pleasant sightseeing and, in an age when people seem constantly to have suffered from pulmonary disorders, was considered the ideal recuperative destination for invalids. For both these groups, Luxor and Aswan, on the Upper Nile, offered 'many good and substantial reasons for wishing to remain some time'. Sightseers found that the surroundings of both centres were rich in pharaonic treasures, while the climate, Cook's declared, was 'superb and highly beneficial to invalids of all kinds'.

To meet this demand, Cook's built the Luxor Hotel in Luxor. It opened in 1877 and, as demand grew, three further hotels were added to the firm's Egyptian empire: the Karnak Hotel in Luxor and the hotels Grand and Cataract in Aswan. This building programme coincided with Cook's commissioning of a fleet of Nile steamers, a departure from the firm's invariable practice elsewhere of acting solely as agent for railway, steamship and hotel owners. This reflected the poor state of the existing facilities in Egypt and also the great importance placed on this area of Cook's business.

The Luxor Hotel, which could accommodate up to 140 people, assured guests that 'unsparing efforts have been made to cater for the creature comforts of visitors and to provide the best food'. It had smoking, reading and writing rooms, a large billiard hall, tennis court and extensive gardens 'so greatly developed and beautified that they are always brilliant with blossoms, yet affording abundant shade'. The hotel was supplied with specially chosen livestock 'fattened for the hotel table', a local dairy provided fresh milk, cream and 'butter churned daily' and the European chefs received their vegetables direct from the hotel's own kitchen garden.

Cook's numerous combination tours frequently included accommodation at the company's hotels. A package offering train travel to Luxor and steamer back to Cairo, for example, included three nights' hotel accommodation in Luxor for £11 15s. An alternative was to take the steamer to and from Luxor and then the train to visit Aswan. The fare of £20 5s included a total of seven nights' stay divided between the two centres.

COOK'S
NILE & PALESTINE
TOURS

Cataract Hotel Assouan.

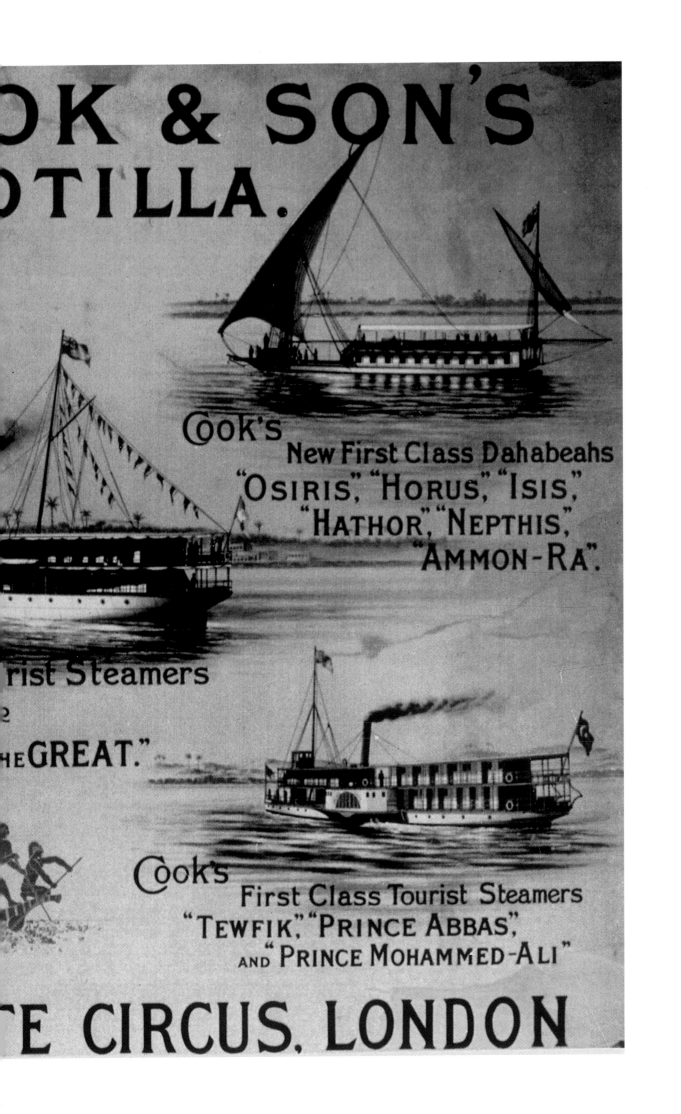

OK & SON'S
OTILLA.

Cook's
New First Class Dahabeahs
"OSIRIS", "HORUS", "ISIS",
"HATHOR", "NEPTHIS",
"AMMON-RA".

rist Steamers

HE GREAT."

Cook's
First Class Tourist Steamers
"TEWFIK", "PRINCE ABBAS",
AND "PRINCE MOHAMMED-ALI"

TE CIRCUS, LONDON

CONQUERING THE HOLY LAND

By 1902, when this handsome advertisement appeared, Cook's had tamed the Holy Land for the tourist. According to a contemporary writer, Cook's had 'the best animals, the best guides, and the best stopping places. Their equipment is first class, and they are as reliable as the Bank of England'. (Coloured)

The pitfalls and problems of organising a trip to Scotland, Switzerland or San Francisco in the 1860s paled into insignificance beside the herculean task that faced Thomas Cook in making the Holy Land accessible to his customers. Here was a region, part of the unstable Ottoman empire, that was without railways or proper roads, had no suitable accommodation and where the principal sights were separated by great stretches of empty desert.

Thomas Cook, placing himself in charge of arrangements, took his first tour party to the Holy Land in 1869. This followed directly on from his first trip to Egypt, but logistically proved far more of a challenge. Cook, having acquired tents and saddles for his party, hired 70 horses to transport them and their equipment. Thirty-three servants were hired to set up camp and attend to the party's needs; two armed guards were employed to protect the group from the very real threat of attack; and, most importantly, Cook carefully selected a dragoman, acting as their guide and interpreter, to lead the group.

Any concerns that Cook's party of around 60 might have had that these difficulties would mean a lowering of standards were soon dispelled. They found that their tents had carpets on the floor, elegant washstands and iron bedsteads supplied with mattresses, proper sheets and blankets. Hearty meals were served by the uniformed servants in a separate tent, with trestle table and chairs, linen tablecloth and gleaming cutlery.

As usual, Cook was not prepared to accept the conditions or facilities that he found in the Holy Land. With his first tour

successfully completed, Cook and his son set about ensuring that their customers received the best horses, harnesses and help that 'practical experience and unstinted expenditure can possibly provide'. The hiring of dragomen was formalised, set itineraries worked out and Cook's usual unimpeachable standards applied.

The most elaborate Middle East tour on offer was Cook's 96-day personally conducted party available at £190. This grand tour travelled via Paris, Milan and Trieste to Egypt, where excursions to the capital's major sights were followed by a 20-day Nile cruise. The party then spent 30 days in the Holy Land, their journey peppered with biblical sights. The itinerary for the second day read: 'Mount horses or leave by carriage; ride through the orange and lemon groves of Jaffa; pass the traditional site where Peter raised Tabitha (Acts ix. 36–41); cross the Plains of Sharon to Ramleh, ascend the Tower, from which is a good view of the whole Plain from the sea to the mountains'. Having worked their way through the main events of the New Testament, the party then made their way home via Constantinople and Athens.

When the German Kaiser, Wilhelm II, wished to tour the Holy Land in 1898 it was natural that he chose John Mason Cook personally to make all the arrangements. This proved to be a huge undertaking. The Kaiser's party consisted of 105 Germans escorted by 27 Ottoman pashas, their entourage and 600 Turkish troops for which 1500 donkeys had to be found. The trip cost the Kaiser £48,130 2s 3d. For John Mason Cook, the cost was even higher: his resistance reduced by the strain of the preparations, he caught dysentery and died at his home in Walton-on-Thames on 4 March 1899.

Appendix

TO

LETTERS FROM THE SEA, &c.

PRELIMINARY NOTICES

OF

FUTURE TOURS

AROUND AND ABOUT THE WORLD.

The object of Mr. COOK, in his Tour Round the World, as indicated by the preceding Letters, has been attained: he has learnt, with great accuracy, the best way Around the Globe; has familiarized himself with the facilities of Travel, by Sea and Land; has noted the chief points of interest, in both hemispheres, where breaks of journey should be made; has found friends, in all lands, who have promised assistance to strangers who may travel under the arrangements which he has inaugurated; has learnt the times and seasons best suited to the Tour; and in conjunction with his co-partners on both sides of the Atlantic, is prepared to state the terms and conditions on which Tours may be made for the entire round, or for partial trips to the East or to the West.

Starting from the Chief Centre of their Tourist operations, at Ludgate Circus, Fleet Street, London,

MESSRS. THOMAS COOK & SON

Can issue Tickets for any part of the United States and for Canada; for the Union and Central Pacific Railroads, with the Branch Lines to Salt Lake City, and from San Francisco to Yosemite Valley and the Big Trees of California; for Yokohama and the Inland Sea of Japan, either for single or double voyages; and in continuation from Shanghai to Hong Kong, Singapore, Penang, Ceylon, Calcutta, the interior of India, Bombay, Aden, Suez, through Egypt to Cairo and Alexandria, and from Alexandria by Brindisi or Venice, and through Italy and France to London; or from Alexandria to Southampton direct, by Gibraltar; or to Naples by sea, and from thence through Italy, and by any route from Italy to London; either direct by Paris or over the Alps and through Switzerland, by the Rhine and through Belgium; or from Italy by the Brenner to Munich, and from thence to London.

Taking the Easterly Route, they can issue Tickets to and through Italy and from Venice, Trieste or Brindisi, to Alexandria or any Port of the Levant, with special arrangements, at the right season, for Tours

through Palestine, Egypt, and up the Nile by steamboats; from Egypt, round by India to China and Japan; returning by the Pacific to San Francisco, through America, and back to London by any line of Atlantic steamers.

These Tickets may be available for twelve months, or longer if desired.

Starting from America,

MESSRS. COOK, SON & JENKINS,

From their Office, 262, BROADWAY, NEW YORK, can issue or arrange for Tickets from any part of the United States, for the Tour Around the World, the same as from London, and for either course—Easterly or Westerly; or for any part of the Tour. They also issue Tickets for individual travellers or parties to visit Great Britain and Ireland, and for every part of the European Continent, or the East.

PERSONALLY-CONDUCTED PARTIES

Are arranged for Tours in any direction, at the proper seasons for the various countries.

Although Messrs. COOK, SON and JENKINS prefer not to arrange for parties to travel through the interior of Palestine in the autumn, they propose arranging for

CHEAP TRIPS FROM LONDON TO JERUSALEM & BACK,

In October and the early part of November; and if found practicable at the time of the visit, to extend the Tours to a few chief places round about Jerusalem, including Bethlehem, the Dead Sea, the Jordan, Jericho, Bethany, &c.

This arrangement will also be made through from America, with facilities at same time of visiting Italy and other Continental countries.

TOURS TO THE NILE IN WINTER, AND TO

PALESTINE IN SPRING,

Will be conducted as heretofore, under the personal supervision of the Messrs. COOK and experienced assistants. For these Tours parties may go in any numbers, at proportionate charges, and the Tours may be for any length of time that parties desire. The arrangements can be extended to the Great Desert and Sinai, and to places East of the Jordan, or from Damascus to the Hauran District.

THE NEXT PERSONALLY-CONDUCTED TOUR

ROUND THE WORLD

Is arranged to leave England at the beginning of September, and it is expected that Mr. ALEXANDER HOWARD, the famous Director of Palestine Tours, will be engaged to accompany the party.

AROUND THE WORLD IN 222 DAYS

Rickshaw, elephant and sedan-chair rides were all on offer to those taking part in Cook's 1891–92 season of round-the-world tours, the company's 20th. (Coloured)

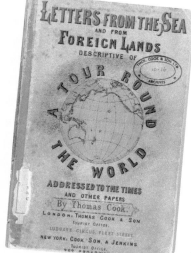

The thought of circumnavigating the globe for pleasure would have been ridiculed even a decade before Thomas Cook led his first party on a round-the-world tour in 1872. Since then there had been great advances in the comfort and speed of the world's steamships, and in 1869 two events crucial to the development of global travel had taken place: on 10 May, the final stake in America's first transcontinental railway was hammered home at Promontory Point, Utah, and on 11 November, the Suez Canal was officially opened.

True to his pioneering instincts, Thomas Cook, who would be voyaging to lands of which he had no personal experience, proposed an inaugural round-the-world trip at a cost of £300. The public were slow to respond to Cook's offer, and it was not until 26 September 1872 that he departed Liverpool with a group of less than a dozen in tow.

The party's route took them to the United States, across the Pacific Ocean to Japan, on to China, Singapore, Ceylon, India and then back through the Suez Canal to Egypt, where the party dispersed. Thomas arrived back home on 6 May 1873, 222 days after departure.

In Cook's absence, Jules Verne had published *Around the world in 80 days,* and this immediately caught the public imagination. By the time this brochure was published, Cook's offered four autumn departure dates from North America (29 August from Vancouver; 15 and 26 September and 8 October from San Francisco) for a 'strictly first-class', fully conducted round-the-world tour. The route was almost identical to that followed by Thomas Cook in 1872. It took almost the same length of time but with, for example, the time of the Atlantic crossing now reduced from 13 to 8 days there was more time to enjoy the sights along the way. The fare was $2100.

With Cook's usual regard for the flexibility of arrangements, prospective travellers were informed that 'the tour can commence and terminate at any point of the circle' with fares adjusted accordingly. Participants from England left Liverpool on 1 August and, after more than a month's conducted tour of the United States, they joined the 15 August sailing from San Francisco. This option cost £450. Alternatively passengers could 'accompany the party as far as convenient, leaving them at some point and rejoining at Yokohama'.

Cook's could also provide circular tickets for independent travellers over any possible route. A ticket, for example, from America via Japan, China, Ceylon, the Suez Canal, Malta, Gibraltar and England was $753, travelling first class. While most customers were content to take their time and enjoy the experience, others used the opportunity to challenge the pace set by Verne's hero, Phileas Fogg. One Englishman, George Griffiths, managed to complete his circumnavigation in only 65 days, a tribute to the golden age of travel.

ŎK'S TOURS
ROUND THE WORLD

FULL STEAM AHEAD

The London and South Western Railway ran services to Hampshire, Dorset and the southwest of England from Waterloo Station, its terminus in the capital since 1848. This 1903 illustration advertised the company's cross-Channel service, which operated between Southampton and Le Havre. (Coloured)

Starting with his simple day trip from Leicester to Loughborough, over lines belonging to the Midland Railway, Thomas Cook made the railways his domain. Anywhere that railways went, Cook soon followed. He depended on the laying of new track to allow his customers to gain access to new regions and the co-operation of the private railway companies to enable him to issue concessionary fares over a variety of different carriers. This co-operation he earned slowly and not without considerable resistance. When Cook attempted to take his excursionists across the English Channel to France in 1855, the Brighton and South Coast Railway refused his business. He was therefore forced to use the Eastern Counties Railway and cross to Europe via Harwich and Antwerp.

By the 1870s, Cook had won his battle. He was allowed to print his own tickets which 'are arranged in small books for each country or route, printed on one side in English and on the other in the language of the country visited'. The discounts he received from the various railway companies he passed on to the public who, Cook believed, would also find his tickets 'the best passport to civility and attention'. Finally the railways themselves benefited as they found that 'travel has increased to an enormous extent over their lines'.

In 1873, Cook, by now the agent of 'every railway line of repute', cemented this symbiotic relationship by publishing the first edition of *Cook's Continental Time Tables*. This one-shilling monthly, its pages packed with every conceivable piece of information, soon established itself as the train traveller's bible. Limiting itself in the beginning to the departures of Europe's railways, steamers and diligences, it soon expanded its coverage to railways further afield. In minute detail it listed the comings and goings of the great and the small, from the Trans-Siberian and the Train Bleu to the Swiss funicular railways and the 6.10 am from London to Bideford.

This timetable, which is now published as two separate volumes, helped the traveller navigate the pitfalls of foreign travel. As well as detailed timetables, it provided information on baggage allowances, insurance, transport of pets and bicycles, location of golf courses, temperatures, time zones and the Jewish, Islamic and Christian Orthodox calendars. Those unsure of how to convert a Russian *verst* or a Swiss *schweizerstunde* into miles had to look no further. While distances could be more problematic than today, passports were far more straightforward. In 1875, Cook's advised that passports were not required by British travellers for most Continental countries, but that it could be 'useful in order to obtain admission to certain Museums'. Where its use was required, a single passport sufficed for an entire family or party travelling together. Applications were to be sent to the Passport Office in Downing Street and should be made 'at least two clear days before the Passport is required'. The cost was two shillings.

THE OFFICES OF THOMAS COOK & SON

This delightful illustration appeared originally in the October 1908 edition of Cook's Traveller's Gazette. *It shows the booking hall in Cook's chief office in London. The caption read: 'Taking tickets at Ludgate Circus. The flight to Egypt: from fog-bound London to cloudless Cairo'.* (Coloured)

When Thomas Cook first moved to his adopted town, Leicester, in September 1841, two months after his inaugural excursion, he took premises at 1 King Street. There he offered his services to the public as a bookseller and printer. Cook's nascent excursion business was just one of a number of sidelines he ran from this residence. He also found time to sell stationery, pens and commemorative medals, to set up a registry office for servants and to dedicate himself to the promotion of the temperance cause.

As important to Cook as the expansion of his system of excursions to other parts of Britain was his part in the construction of the 1700-seat Temperance Hall that opened in Leicester in 1853. Next door, at 63 Granby Street, he started up Cook's Commercial and Family Temperance Hotel. His excursion business had another new office.

In 1854, Cook finally gave up general printing to devote himself full time to tourism, but his financial standing continued to be precarious. The Leicester boarding house, capably run by his wife, Marianne, provided a steady income to help even out the fickle receipts from Cook's tours. Similarly, when Thomas Cook moved to London in 1862, his wife opened the British Museum Boarding House at 59 Great Russell Street, while he planned out his tours in the building's conservatory.

Finally, in 1865, Cook was in a position to open his first official London office, located at 98 Fleet Street. To supplement the takings, his wife and daughter operated a temperance boarding house on the upper storey, while his son, who ran the

office with the help of one assistant and an office boy, also sold travel paraphernalia and guidebooks.

For more than half a century, Ludgate Circus had only one association in the public mind. In 1873, this busy intersection at the end of Fleet Street became the site of Thomas Cook & Son's head office. John Mason Cook later admitted that 'it was thought impossible for us ever to require premises of such magnitude'. Initially, a portion of the ground floor was occupied by a branch Post Office and one of the Midland Railway's goods-receiving offices, and the upper floors had to be sublet.

As the company continued to grow, Cook's 'found the absolute necessity of occupying the whole of the building'. The ground floor was given over to the Public Booking Office, the Banking and Exchange Department and the Shipping Department. The basement was used to store travellers' baggage; the mezzanine included the office of John Mason Cook and the Reading Room, 'a spacious and comfortable apartment for the free use of our Travelers and Visitors'. On the upper three floors were the offices of John Mason Cook's sons and the staff of the Banking, Accounts, and Audits and Rates Departments.

From this central nerve-centre, instructions passed around the world to the steadily growing network of Cook's offices. When the company celebrated its Golden Jubilee in 1891, John Mason Cook proudly announced that Thomas Cook now had 84 offices (including 11 in London), 85 agencies and 2692 staff. They stretched from Brussels (opened 1869), Cairo (1872), Chicago (1873) and Paris (1874) to Beirut (1881), Bombay (1881), Sydney (1888) and Rangoon (1890).

CASH IN HAND

In the constant retelling of Cook's history, fact and fiction frequently merged. This 1930s poster, for instance, incorrectly dates Cook's traveller's cheques back to 1871 rather than 1874. It also shows a miniaturised version of Cook's new Berkeley Street headquarters, which opened in 1926 and included expansive facilities for the Banking and Foreign Exchange Department.

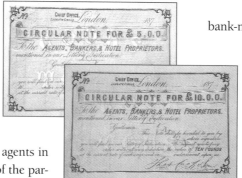

'For many years past', Thomas Cook wrote in 1874, 'we have been urged by great numbers of the passengers availing themselves of our tickets and hotel coupons, to allow them to deposit their surplus money with us, and give them some medium by which they would be enabled to draw it from our agents in various parts of the world, in the currency of the particular country where they happened to require it'.

Cook had, until then, been forced to decline these entreaties due to the lack of any appropriate 'machinery'. The success of his hotel coupon system, launched in 1868, and the growth in the number of international offices had finally given Cook the necessary network of encashment points to make a system of traveller's money viable. Cook duly launched his first traveller's cheques, which he christened Circular Notes, in New York in 1874.

As usual, Cook took meticulous care to ensure the smooth operation of his new venture. Hand-written letters were sent to all potential places of encashment introducing the scheme, enclosing samples and requesting them 'to kindly accept our Notes in the same way you accept the Notes of English Bankers'. The original Circular Notes, available in £5 and £10 denominations, were valid for 12 months from the date of issuance and required only a single signature to be cashed. As a means of identification, and of verifying this signature, Cook's issued each Note holder with a Letter of Indication. This contained the all-important sample signature, as well as a record of the cheques issued and a full list of the places where the Notes could be cashed.

The great success of Cook's Circular Notes led to the establishment of a separate Banking Department in 1878. It advised its customers never to carry 'surplus funds in the form of bank-notes, in consequence of the losses by theft which frequently occur' and worked to extend the utility of the Circular Note. Cook's branches around the world received a steady stream of correspondence from the head office in London regarding changes to the design and denomination of the Circular Notes, and this was followed in the 1890s by a booklet detailing the correct method of endorsing cheques, the exact procedure for telegraphic remittances and an important note on identification. If, for example, instructions were received to hand over Circular Notes to a specified individual, it was incumbent upon the clerk on duty to confirm the identity of the applicant. The booklet advised that 'this can be done by producing passport, letters addressed to him, or by showing the name marked on cuffs, etc'.

In 1905, in response to complaints that sterling Notes were 'not found to be very convenient for use in the Western States of America', Cook's introduced its first series of dollar Circular Notes in amounts of $25 and $50. This was followed in 1909 by the decision to adopt the name traveller's cheque, a term used by American Express since its own circular notes were introduced in 1891. A further innovation was the introduction in 1929 of the self-identifying cheque. The cheque was signed on purchase and countersigned on presentation, thus ending the need for the Letter of Indication.

A system begun as a service to its customers had evolved into an important source of revenue for Cook's and it was proud to announce that thanks to Cook's traveller's cheques the tourist abroad 'can be carefree with plenty of money in his pocket-money that is mere paper to anybody else, whether thief, forger, or dishonest finder'.

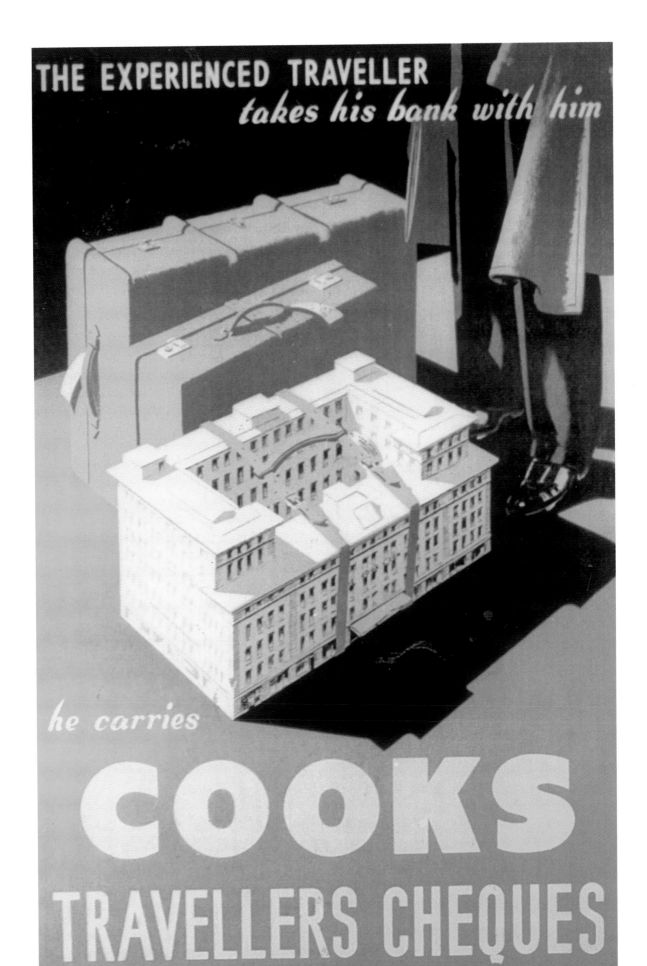

THE LAND OF THE MIDNIGHT SUN

The dominant theme of this 1892 travel brochure is the scenic wonders awaiting the independent traveller in Scandinavia. 'An expeditious traveller,' it advised, 'can leave Hull, catch the steamer at Bergen or Trondhjem, go to the North Cape, and be back in London within twenty days'. (Coloured)

The shelves in a modern travel agent are packed with row upon row of attractive brochures, their pages full of happy people enjoying the perfect weather and the unforgettable sights of an unmissable destination. In brochureland, the colours are brighter, the people friendlier, the prices cheaper and the hotel bedrooms certainly bigger. This is nothing new.

Throughout the 19th century, Cook's produced countless brochures and endless publicity material to promote its tours and services. Instead of the glossy colour photograph, Cook's used the power of the pen to portray the endless charms of the chosen location. In Cookland, the British are always slightly superior, the country in question somewhat less sophisticated and the customs somehow more backward than at home.

Scandinavia had first been introduced to Cook's tourists in 1875 as a summer resort. Scandinavia really meant Norway, the 'Land of the Midnight Sun', with Sweden and Denmark as complementary sideshows. Norway's great selling point was its exceptional and unspoilt natural beauty, though this was seriously understating the case. This 1892 brochure, which gave sample itineraries and information on touring in northern Europe, eulogised as follows: 'No country within such easy reach of England can for a moment compare with Norway in the variety and beauty of its scenery, in the bracing and health-giving qualities of its climate, and in all the features that provide the traveller with complete change of air and scene for which so many visit foreign lands'.

For such an undeveloped nation, Norway gained fulsome praise: 'The food is good as a rule, if somewhat limited in variety . . . In all the large towns really good hotels exist . . . The beer of the country is excellent . . . The roads are marvels of engineering skill . . . There is also much in the people themselves, their cities, their homes, and their habits, that well deserves to be noted'. Even Norway's lack of civilised amenities was seen as a benefit: 'There are no picture galleries to make one's neck ache; no museums to make the weary feet throb; no promenades; no sherry cobblers to sip while bands play in the gardens'. On top of all this, Norway offered the traveller the chance to experience a fascinating natural phenomenon: 'There is no night in Norway during June, July, and August, and the glorious light-effects that may be seen are an education in colour, and an endless delight to the eye. But the climax is to see the midnight sun in its glory, and this can only be enjoyed by the traveller when well within the Arctic circle'.

Thomas Cook & Son offered the independent traveller a bewildering variety of possible routes to Scandinavia. A steamer, for instance, direct to Copenhagen cost £2 10s, to Bergen £4 and Oslo (then called Christiana) £4 4s. Alternatively, Cook's offered circular tickets, valid for 30 days, that covered transport over a chosen route by a combination of steamboat, railway and, for remoter areas, Cook's fleet of specially constructed horse-drawn conveyances (*carrioles, stolkjärres* and landaus). One of the less complicated options was as follows: from London to Christiana by the Wilson line, railway to Eidsvold, steamer on Lake Mjösen to Hamar and Gjövik, *carriole* to Odnaes, steamer to Randsfjord, then by rail to Hönefos, Drammen and back to Christiana, before returning to London. The fare was £7 16s 9d first class, £5 13s second class.

MOUNTING VESUVIUS

Overleaf, a souvenir postcard shows the horse-drawn carriage that transported passengers from Naples to the foot of Mount Vesuvius and the funicular that took them up the side of the volcano. It was posted on 5 August 1902 and addressed to José Guedes in Lisbon, Portugal.

A visit to Pompeii and the smouldering volcano nearby that had been responsible for burying the town in ash in AD 79 was one of the highlights of any Victorian visit to southern Italy. Ascending the mountainside, however, could wreak havoc on a lady's raiment and so, sensing an opportunity for profit, Ernesto Emmanuele Oblieght, a Hungarian tramway promoter, opened a funicular there in 1880.

The early fate of the mountain railway proved the gulf that existed between a profitable idea and its successful implementation. The service almost immediately ran into financial difficulties and so John Mason Cook, realising its value to his customers, decided to buy it in 1887. This one small railway, only 896 metres in length, proved to be as much trouble as an entire network.

Cook immediately ran into the opposition of local guides, who tried to dictate terms to him. When he refused to accept their inflated prices, they resorted to sabotaging the track and burning down one of the stations. It is a testament to Cook's tenacity that he persisted and, by the 1890s, the funicular was returning a handsome profit of about £2000 a year.

For an all-inclusive fare of 25 francs, *Cook's Excursionist* explained, passengers 'are conveyed to the crater without any inconvenience, annoyance or fatigue . . . Carriages leave our

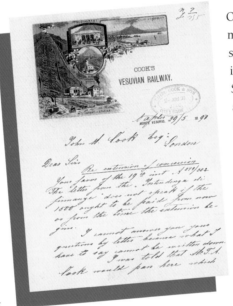

Offices, Piazza dei Martiri, Naples, every morning, Sundays excepted, for large or small parties, at an inclusive fare, providing for a drive through the City and Suburbs of Naples . . . to the Restaurant and Railway Station, at the foot of the cone, then from the Lower to the Upper Stations by Funicular Train to within 150 yards of the crater'. From here the repentant guides were on hand to escort passengers to the very top. Cook's even advertised: 'Any passengers, through physical weakness, requiring special help can be provided with an extra guide or with a "chaise à porteur" at a fixed moderate price'.

Cook also set about improving the equipment and, before his death, authorised the construction of a five-mile-long electric railway providing access from Naples. But the mountain played its part in trying to disrupt Cook's investment. An eruption in 1906 destroyed the upper part of the track and coated the entire area with ash. Again the funicular was restored and remained part of the Thomas Cook empire until 1945, when it was sold for 3.1 million lire.

For the tourist, unaware of these difficulties, the funicular continued to be a welcome aid to scaling Vesuvius. 'We have a lovely day', wrote a happy sightseer on a postcard dated 8 April 1901, 'and it is a sight I shall never forget looking into the enormous crater'.

THOS COOK & SON
· NAPLES ·

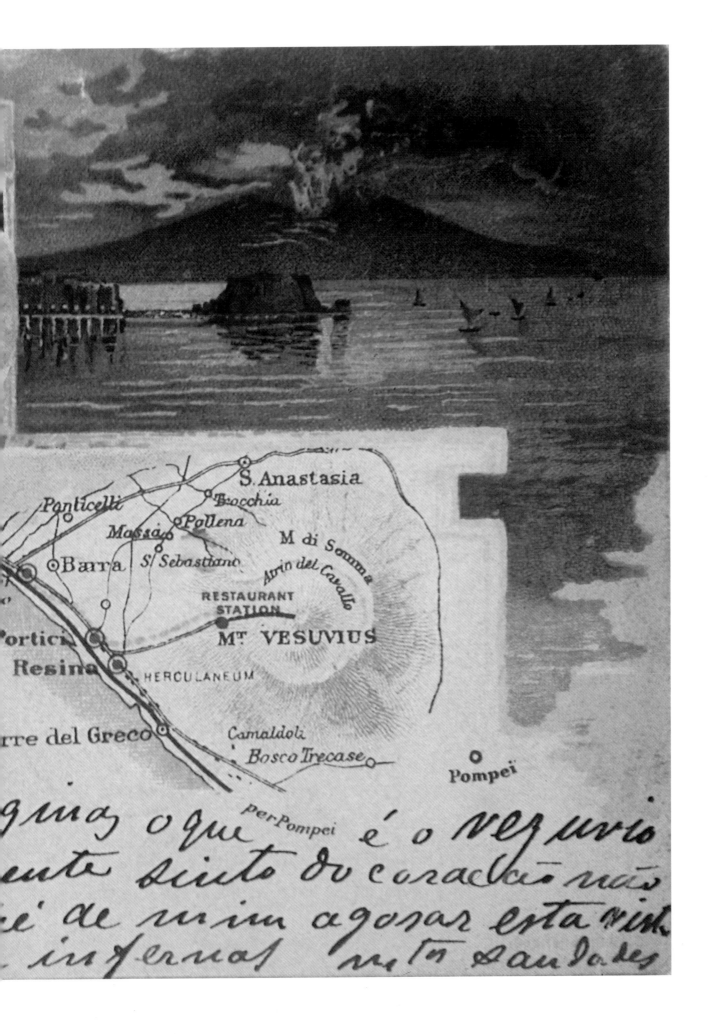

A WINTER WONDERLAND

'No one can be said to really know Switzerland', advised the brochure for Cook's 1908–09 winter-season arrangements, *'who has not seen it in winter'*. (Coloured)

Winter Sports
Season 1923-4
THOS. COOK & SON.

It is said to have begun with a bet. The English traditionally travelled to Switzerland during the cool summer months. In the winter, fashionable society migrated to the warm Mediterranean lands which is when the Côte d'Azur and Egypt had their 'season'. The concept of sunbathing was unheard of until the 1920s; winter sports were equally unknown and most Swiss hotels and restaurants closed during the off-season.

In September 1864, a hotel owner in St Moritz by the name of Johannes Badrutt supposedly made a wager with four English guests. He wanted to put their preconceptions about the bleakness of an alpine winter to the test. If they would return to his hotel later that year they would find that in Switzerland in winter the sun frequently shone and the scenery acquired a new beauty. If they were not suitably impressed, he promised to pay all their expenses and allow them to return to London at once; if they found it to their liking, then they must agree to stay, though at no charge, until spring. Needless to say they liked what they found and so the Swiss winter season got its first free publicity.

From then on, increasing numbers, led by the redoubtable English, began to visit Switzerland in winter. Thomas Cook, whose own first foray into what he called 'the mountain home of liberty' had taken place in the summer of 1863, first offered winter tours to the public in the 1880s. With this growing influx of visitors also came the vogue for winter sports, which was eloquently explained in his 1908 brochure: 'there yet remains a new pleasure in life. Winter sport exhilarates and rejuvenates; it generates a glow of pleasure in the mind, which acts powerfully upon the whole physical organisation, while all the time the nerves and muscles are directly braced up by the keen, dry air, tempered by bright, genial sunshine'.

The main centres for Cook's winter tourists at this time were Adelboden, Andermatt, Engelberg, Grindelwald, St Moritz and Samaden. During the day visitors could enjoy a wide range of sports, with skating, bobsleigh and skiing among the most popular. Hotels organised ice gymkhanas, sleigh excursions and curling competitions, and, at night, the warm clothes were replaced by evening wear as guests enjoyed grand concerts, fancy-dress balls and amateur theatricals.

Each resort had its own cachet and Cook's priced its winter-sports packages accordingly. St Moritz was the most prestigious centre and a ticket, providing escorted second-class travel there and back and one week's full board and lodging at the Hotel Belvedere, cost from £11, 'according to the room selected'. The cheapest destination was Engelberg, where travel and a room at the centrally heated Grand Winterhaus or Kuranstalt Hotel cost £9 10s. Cook's made only one stipulation regarding its winter sports programme: 'no visitors who are suffering from any form of tubercular complaint are received at the places dealt with in this booklet'.

SUNSHINE AND SNOW.

Winter Sports in SWITZERLAND

SYNOPSIS OF ARRANGEMENTS
MADE BY

THOS COOK & SON,
Ludgate Circus,
LONDON,
E.C.

Season 1908~9.

INNOCENTS ABROAD

This redesigned cover of Cook's Excursionist, *American Edition, was introduced in 1884. To the left of the title is a picture of Cook's main American office at 261 Broadway, New York.* (Coloured)

Thomas Cook, after successfully arranging a series of tours from Britain to the United States in the 1860s, undertook to persuade Americans in turn to use his organisation to travel abroad. In 1873, as part of this initiative, Cook began publication of an American edition of his well-established *Cook's Excursionist.* Through this medium, printed monthly and priced at 10 cents, Cook sought to educate the readership 'who, though familiar with the title "Cook's Tours," are yet unfamiliar with our system'. Cook went out of his way to dispel the misunderstanding of potential customers who 'are under the impression that in order to travel under our arrangements they are obliged to do so in parties'. Concerns about cost should also not put people off, as Cook believed that 'it is often easier and cheaper to spend a summer abroad than to stay at home'.

The *Excursionist* acknowledged that 'Few people who have not travelled under our arrangements are aware of the many facilities we afford to travelers and the vast extent of our connections'. Accordingly, the reader was conducted through the world of Thomas Cook & Son and there discovered that: 'to-day Cook's Tickets are found in use in nearly every country where civilization has exerted its influence sufficiently to provide the means of transport and protection for travelers'.

Cook also aimed to reassure his readers about the conditions they would encounter at journey's end and thus each issue provided a list of 'Useful hints for tourists'. First things first. In 1884 the column advised would-be passengers that 'Passports are not at present absolutely necessary for American travelers in Europe, except for visiting Russia, Turkey, Egypt, Spain or Portugal'. Next on to baggage. 'A strong medium-sized wooden or leather trunk is preferable – it should be of simple construction, so that it can be opened in an instant for Custom's Examination, and possess a good lock . . . Trunks should in all cases bear the name or initials of the owner painted in plain letters at the top or on the sides for ready identification'. Other suggested accessories included 'a small field or large opera glass', a pocket compass, a scrapbook, toilet soap, a sewing kit and 'a package or two of address or visiting cards'.

There was also a note on medicines. 'It is not our vocation to prescribe, but aperient or astringent medicines may be required, and quinine is not unfrequently [sic] of use . . . A little court-plaster, extract of ginger, ammonia, arnica, or some kind of liniment enter into every tourist's outfit'. Finally on to the troublesome issue of language. Cook's reassured its American clientele: 'English is spoken by almost all the hotel-keepers, waiter and merchants throughout the Continent, and interpreters are to be found at the railway stations, so that ignorance of foreign languages is no longer a valid excuse for stopping home. The *numerals* in French, German and Italian can be easily learned, also a few useful phrases'.

Suitably forewarned and forearmed, Cook's American reader was then inundated with the list of possible tours available from Cook's offices. Domestic tours to the Catskills and a grand tour to California, Colorado and the Yosemite Valley appeared alongside offers of trips to Bermuda, the Windward Islands, Cuba and Mexico. As the readers, gaining in confidence, progressed through the publication's pages, they moved even further afield. Cook's 1884 May Party to Europe, lasting three and a half months, was available for $650, including the journey to England. Ten weeks in Spain and Algeria cost $500 and, for a real splurge, a 100-day grand tour of Scandinavia, Russia and central Europe was offered at a price of $850.

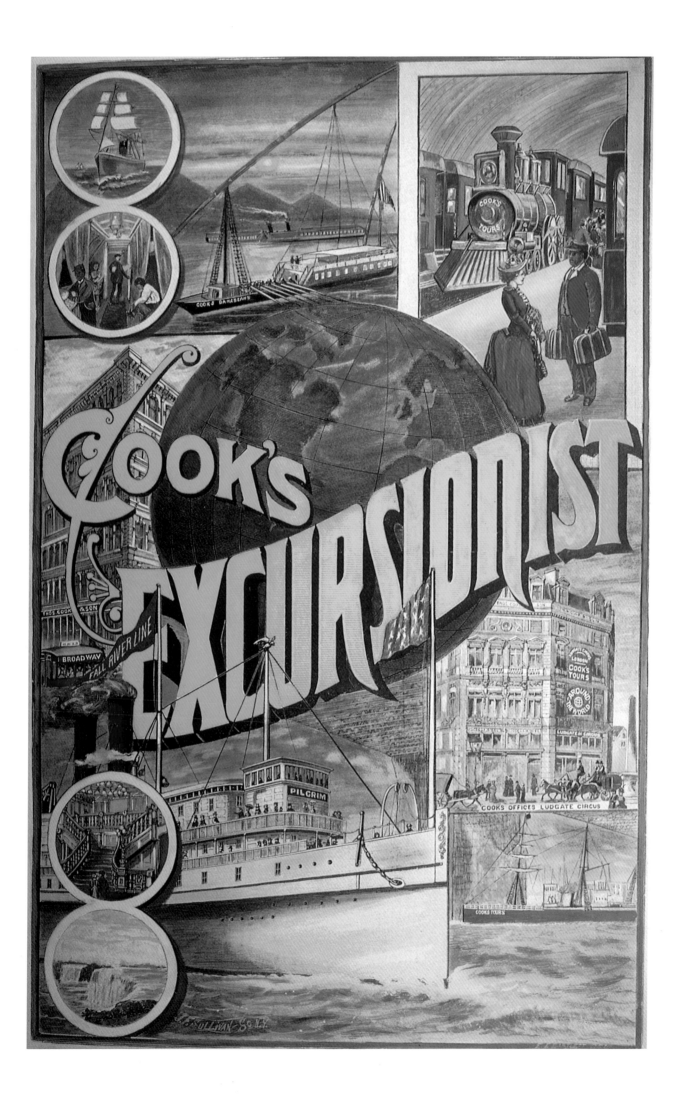

THE JEWEL IN THE CROWN

This colourful procession adorned the pamphlet advertising Cook's fully escorted tour of India, Ceylon and Burma leaving London on 22 December 1939. The 120-day tour cost £402 and was to include visits to Colombo, Rangoon, Agra, Darjeeling and Bombay. With the outbreak of war in August 1939, it is unlikely that the tour ever took place.

British India, the jewel in the crown of the empire, was one of the regions that received its first visit from a member of the Cook family during Thomas's pioneering round-the-world tour of 1872–73. Before leaving England, Cook had written that his desire in India was to 'see how the influences of Anglican society, government, and Christian and philanthropic efforts, show themselves'. He duly spent his six weeks on the sub-continent concerned more with the civilising work of Baptist missionaries than with investigating the region's tourist potential. While his party spent their time viewing Mogul monuments, Cook gave a lecture to the British garrison at Agra on his own experience of teetotalism.

Where Thomas Cook went his son soon followed, although this time the interests of the business were paramount. During John Mason Cook's 1881 visit, he set up the company's first Indian office in Bombay, he courted senior government officials and negotiated special rates with railway officials. On his return, India was officially added to Cook's travel empire with the publication of a shilling brochure entitled Cook's Indian Tours. It contained an extensive programme of tours and numerous tips for the first-time visitor. A typical three-month ticket, starting in London, travelling by P&O steamer and including visits to Bombay, Calcutta, Darjeeling, Benares, Delhi and Lahore, cost £113 7s in first class, £66 4s in second. The guide advised: 'Travellers will find it desirable to engage a native servant during their stay in India, but should be cautious in their selection. None but well-known men should be employed, as certificates are easily borrowed, and cannot be always relied upon'. A circular ticket from Bombay, valid for two months and following the same route as above, cost

143.30 rupees for first class, 71.10 rupees in second and 24.12 rupees for any accompanying native servant. The guide also included a helpful Hindi glossary, with essential phrases such as 'Take my boots off' and 'Are there alligators in this river?'

The number of tourists visiting India was initially small, but Cook's position was enhanced by several official commissions. In 1887, the firm was invited to make arrangements for senior British officials and Indian princes to attend Queen Victoria's Golden Jubilee celebrations in London. Making travel arrangements for maharajas and nabobs presented Cook's staff with unique difficulties (one prince insisted on travelling with 200 servants, 50 family attendants, 20 chefs, 10 elephants, 33 tigers, 1000 packing cases and a small howitzer) and so in the 1890s Cook's set up the Indian Princes Department. Also in 1887, following overtures from the viceroy, Cook's began organising the transport of Indian Muslims on the annual pilgrimage to Mecca. They had previously been subjected to terrible conditions and extortions, and Cook's brought welcome order to the proceedings. The agreement was terminated by the Indian Government in 1893.

India, as with so many destinations before and after, had been fully absorbed into Cook's global travel system. A country that had originally offered little help to the curious sightseer had been tamed by Cook's system of tickets and coupons, and by its constant efforts to improve tourist facilities. The viceroy may have ruled India politically but, at the ports and stations and tourist bungalows, Cook was the undisputed raja.

Select Escorted Tour of
CEYLON, BURMA &
INDIA

LEAVING LONDON DECEMBER 22nd, 1939
and MARSEILLES DECEMBER 30th, 1939

HOMEWARD BOUND

Cook's Oriental Traveller's Gazette *first appeared in 1889 and was published monthly at a cost of four annas. It was available post free anywhere in India or Burma.* (Coloured)

Despite the apparent misnomer of its title, *Cook's Oriental Traveller's Gazette* was printed each month in Bombay and was aimed specifically at the civil servants, officials and military personnel living in Britain's Indian empire. For these Anglo-Indians (the term had not yet come to mean someone of mixed race), the main focus of their travel ambitions was what to do with their lengthy 'home leave'. For most it was simply a case of returning directly to Blighty, and each issue of *Cook's Oriental Traveller's Gazette* was dominated by the lists of 'Fares for through single and return tickets between India and London'.

The Peninsular & Oriental Steam Navigation Company, founded in 1837, had become the pukka way to travel to and from Britain's eastern possessions. Its India service had even given rise to a new term for first-class travel: posh. Travelling out from England, across the Red Sea and the Indian Ocean, the coolest, and hence the most desirable, cabins were on the northern side of the ship and similarly on the journey home. Customers therefore demanded a POSH ticket: Port Out, Starboard Home. Through the offices of Thomas Cook & Son such tickets, valid for a return journey within three months, were available for 1000 rupees, or 1150 rupees for passengers opting to return on the faster mail route, which meant first travelling

overland to Brindisi. Second-class tickets cost 600 and 690 rupees respectively. Native servants could be taken for an additional 300 rupees. Tickets were also available for the sailings of the other major steamship companies, including: Florio-Rubattino and Austrian Lloyds from Bombay, the Clan, British India and Star lines out of Calcutta, the Hall Line from Karachi and the Bibby Line from Rangoon.

Cook's sought to entice the more adventurous reader to detour on their way home, and the *Oriental Traveller's Gazette* consequently advertised tickets to every destination imaginable, from Adelaide to Zanzibar. The Gazette also reproduced a selection of itineraries for tours 'From India to Europe via China, Japan, America, Canada and Australia'. A specially reduced rate was offered to 'Missionaries and Officers (and their Families) of the British, and Foreign Military, Naval and Civil Services, who book through to Liverpool or London'. For 1151 rupees, the returning Anglo-Indian could travel to Penang, Singapore and Hong Kong by P&O and then on to Yokohama and the delights of Japan, cross the Pacific to San Francisco, traverse the United States with stops at 'all places of interest' and finally board an England-bound liner in New York.

COOK'S ORIENTAL TRAVELLERS' GAZETTE

AND HOME & FOREIGN ADVERTISER

LONDON

COOKS OFFICE

ROME

PARIS

AGRA

VICTORIA STATION, BOMBAY.

FROM SAIGON TO SURABAYA

Thomas Cook & Son chose a traditional shadow puppet, used in Malaysia's wayang kulit plays, to adorn the front of this 1926 brochure cover.

Somerset Maugham's short stories provide a delightful image of life in the eastern outposts of empire in the inter-war years. Amid the rubber plantations and isolated jungle homesteads, his characters live lives that are peppered with intrigue and dark secrets. Maugham gained this insight from his own travels in the region, but he was not always enamoured by what he saw. On visiting Bangkok in 1923 he wrote: 'It is impossible to consider these populous modern cities of the East without a certain malaise. They are all alike with their straight streets, their arcades, their tramways, their dust, their blinding sun, their teeming Chinese, their dense traffic, their ceaseless din'. Cook's view was very different.

Thomas Cook & Son's first office in Singapore opened in 1922, and promotional brochures such as this were produced in order to encourage travel in the region, both among overseas visitors and the expatriates who provided Maugham with such rich material for his tales. This particular brochure is devoid of prices. Its intention was to inform visitors of the range of possibilities on offer. For the uninformed traveller here was proof that the omnipresent Cook's organisation reached into even the remotest islands of the Dutch East Indies, through the most impenetrable Siamese jungle and to every tourist site of note throughout French Indo-China and the Malay States.

Where train lines existed, Cook's had acquired the agency; where they did not, a fleet of 'dependable and up-to-date' cars were on hand to provide transport over 'the 3500 miles of magnificent roads through the plantations, jungle and mountains of the peninsula'. Cook's hotel coupons were accepted at all the region's finest hotels, including the Oriental in Bangkok, Raffles in Singapore and Batavia's Hotel des Indes. Cook's traveller's cheques could be cashed at all the major centres. Cook's had even cornered the market in guides. As the brochure modestly pointed out, in some areas 'English-speaking guides are few . . . The one or two who can explain "things" in English are employed by Cook's for their "Inclusive Tour" clients'.

In short, 'Cook's knowledge of the principal places of interest to the traveller, and the resources at their disposal in what is a new country from the standpoint of tourism, are, it is believed, unapproached by any other travel organisation'. The world was a smaller place thanks to Thomas Cook & Son. A visit to Wonosobo, Ipoh, Bentong, Bukit Fraser, Djockja, Tosari or Quihon was now no more difficult than a trip to Calais, Karlsruhe or the Swiss cantons.

MALAYSIA
AND
INDO-CHINA

THOS. COOK & SON LTD.

THE INSCRUTABLE ORIENT

A 1917 brochure advertises Cook's tours to the Far East. The picture typifies western perceptions of Japan at this time, which the brochure described as 'the land of quaint temples, pagodas and shrines, Geishas and flower festivals'.

The *jinrikisha* (literally 'human-powered vehicle'), synonymous with Japan and the Far East, was in fact invented by an American Baptist missionary. The Rev Jonathan Scobie devised this unique conveyance in 1869 to transport his invalid wife around the streets of Yokohama. In a country emerging from more than two centuries of isolation, where labour was cheap and there was no railway until 1877, rickshaws (as the ignorant tourist called them) provided the first public-transportation system. By the end of 1871, 15,000 were registered in Tokyo alone; 40,000 by the following year. For the Japanese, they were a practical means of getting around; for the tourist they were an indelible symbol of this quintessentially oriental nation.

Thomas Cook, when he first visited Japan in 1872, declared that the rickshaw 'is of itself one of the wonders of the country . . . I was so amused and pleased with this novel Japanese institution, that I have ordered a specimen copy to be shipped to London (but without the coolie)'. (It is now in Leicester's Newarke Houses Museum). Future Cook's tourists were assured that rickshaws 'are placed daily at the disposal of our guests'.

The rickshaw spread around Asia, to Shanghai, Manila, Singapore and Calcutta, with the same rapidity as the public's growing fascination with the Far East. Some westerners were content to collect Oriental art and curios from afar, while others felt drawn to visit these developing nations in person. Among the latter was Rudyard Kipling. In 1889 he returned to England from India via the Far East. Japan made a lasting impression on him and, after his marriage to Carrie Balestier in 1892, he returned there with his wife as part of an intended round-the-world voyage. Kipling had the good sense to make his travel arrangements through Thomas Cook, because the failure of the Oriental Banking Company while he was in Yokohama left him stranded and without funds. Cook's agent arranged for the unused portion of their tickets to be refunded and organised direct passage for them back to London.

In 1917, despite the bloody conflict raging in Europe, the Far East seemed an unspoilt region whose people, the brochure assured its readers, 'have preserved unchanged through thousands of years the same curious usages, archaic appliances and surroundings'. A 114-day tour from San Francisco, encompassing Honolulu, the Philippines, China, Manchuria, Korea and Japan, cost $1425; a 60-day visit to see Japan during the cherry-blossom season was $750. In all instances, Cook's assured its customers that 'Our Tour Managers are gentlemen of experience and tact, familiar with the routes and conditions, and their efforts, with the assistance of our many Resident Agents and the best local guides, are devoted to obtaining for our patrons a thoroughly enjoyable, satisfactory and interesting journey'.

JAPAN CHINA
THE PHILIPPINES

THOS. COOK & SON

COOK REDISCOVERS THE ANTIPODES

Another addition to Cook's range of travel publications, Cook's Australasian Traveller's Gazette, *a two-penny monthly, was first issued in 1889.* (Coloured)

While bringing the whole world of Cook's travel to its readers, each foreign edition of the *Traveller's Gazette* was also designed to cater to the tastes and interests of those in the region in which it circulated. The huge size and relative isolation of the two southern-most of England's 19th-century colonies meant that *Cook's Australasian Traveller's Gazette* concentrated on tours within Australia and New Zealand and throughout the Pacific. The cover of the *Gazette* reproduced here, with its montage of local scenes, reflects this preoccupation.

Today's Australian states were then separate colonies and Cook's hoped that its travel arrangements 'will be found to offer great inducements to those wishing to extend their holiday trips across the borders of their respective colonies'. Cook's believed that by travelling to Sydney, a resident of Victoria colony would come to appreciate 'the wealth of lovely scenery possessed by New South Wales, the facilities for visiting the National Park, Illawara district, Fitzroy Falls, Blue Mountains, Hawkesbury River, Lake Macquarie, and other favorite resorts from Sydney being cheap and abundant'.

This parochialism made a visit to New Zealand a significant undertaking that Thomas Cook & Son was happy to organise.

In 1892, for a payment of £25, the traveller from Australia received a combined ticket as follows: 'Union S.S. Company, Melbourne to Wellington via the Bluff, Dunedin and Lyttelton (Christchurch); rail Wellington to Napier; coach to Taupo and Wairakei, including guide fee for sights at Wairakei; coach to Rotorua (for Hot Lakes), buggies, guides and all fees included for Waiotapu Valley, Whakarewarewa and Tikitere, and launch on Lake Rotorua; coach to Oxford; rail to Auckland; thence steamer to Sydney. First class'.

That same year Cook's had 'pleasure in announcing' its third annual escorted party to China and Japan. The fare for this three-month adventure, with 'everything strictly first-class', was £140, a deposit of £25 payable 'as early as possible'. According to the itinerary printed in the *Gazette* the group would leave Sydney on board the *Airlie*, 'a fine roomy ship of 2336 tons', on 1 March 1892, arrive at Darwin 12 days later (passing 'an abundance of charming scenery' on the way) and finally reach 'the fine harbour of HONGKONG' on 23 March. Here the visitor was promised that 'innumerable phases of Chinese life and character may be studied, especially in the native portion'.

The party, having had their first taste of the Orient, spent another 10 days reaching the main object of their voyage: Japan. The tour was now warned: 'While travelling in the interior of Japan the luggage must be reduced to small packages, such as hand-bags and travelling rugs, there being no possibility of carrying trunks along with the party'. As well as visits to Tokyo, Osaka, Kobe, Nagasaki and Nikko, four days were devoted to the ancient capital of Kyoto 'where there will be found an endless variety of sights to engage attention, including the fantastically designed temples, lovely gardens, manufactories and workshops, porcelain and pottery works, curio. shops, theatres, acrobatic exhibitions, and wrestling matches. The trips from the city will include a trip of sixteen miles through beautiful country, in jinrickshas'.

To ensure participants got maximum value for their money, the party stopped on the way home at Canton, China and Sandakan in British North Borneo. On 12 June, 104 days after setting sail, the *Airlie* arrived home in Sydney.

Cook's Australasian Travellers Gazette

Milford Sound N3

Bendlan Caves N.S.W

Cape Raoul Tas

WESTERN AUSTRALIA

Queensland

King William St Adelaide

Port Phillip Heads Vic.

INTO AFRICA

The nature reserves of East Africa beckon. The cover of this 1936 brochure shows a reproduction of an oil painting by Major A Radclyffe Dugmore entitled A pair of kings.

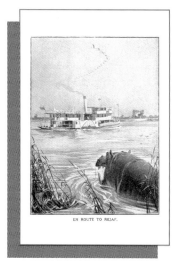

EN ROUTE TO REJAF.

In April 1909, 14 years after a reluctant British government had declared British East Africa a protectorate, Theodore Roosevelt, ex-president of the United States, and his son, Kermit, landed in Mombasa at the start of an epic 11-month safari that was to place the new colonial possession firmly on the travel map. A delighted Roosevelt, who personally shot 296 'specimens' during his trip, including 9 lions, 8 elephants, 15 zebra, 3 python and a baboon, declared the country 'an ideal playground alike for sportsmen and travellers'. Kenya Colony (as it was redesignated in 1920) had a white population of just some 5500 and only the single-track Uganda Railway, known as the Lunatic Line, linking the coast with the interior, but its natural splendours and abundant game made it a popular destination among Cook's wealthier patrons.

Thomas Cook & Son opened its first branch offices in the colony, in Nairobi and Mombasa, in 1933, and offered a remarkable array of motor tours run by 'a permanent staff of thoroughly trustworthy European drivers and mechanics'. For the short-term visitor the options included a one and a half hour tour of the environs of Mombasa (6s per person for a party of two; 4s for a group of four) or, for those whose steamer stopped to refuel at Mombasa, a two-day excursion to the capital, Nairobi, including a sightseeing drive (£11 5s per person for first-class travel and hotel, £9 11s in second class).

Those with longer to spend exploring could opt for an eight-day circular tour from Nairobi, visiting the Masai Reserve, Kilimanjaro, Arusha and Ngorongoro, with prices starting at £29 2s. Then there was the inevitable safari. Six days camping in the big-game country of the Serengeti with two cars, petrol and six servants cost £45 each for two persons. By the 1930s, most tourists were happy only to shoot the wildlife with their cameras, but Cook's advised that a Big Game Licence was available for an extra £10.

As usual, Cook's brochures were also full of helpful tips for the would-be traveller. In the matter of clothing, it offered this advice. 'Ordinary summer or light-weight clothing is suitable for travel in the Highland areas, and practically everything needed can be purchased in Nairobi, Mombasa and other large centres in East Africa. A warm overcoat is often welcome in the higher altitudes. A solar topee is indispensable, as everywhere in the tropics, and should be worn between the hours of 8 am and 4 pm'.

Travel in East Africa

COOK'S HANDBOOK

A.R Dugmore

RIDING RHODES' RAILS

This 1907 illustration, also used on brochure covers, shows the Victoria Falls and the perceived advantages brought to southern Africa by the railways. (Coloured)

Diamonds, gold and Cecil Rhodes made South Africa a talking point; the Boer War of 1899–1902 ingrained it in the British conscience. A country that once held little interest to the casual visitor now became a must-see. In 1900, Thomas Cook & Son opened its first office in Cape Town and Cook's tourists soon followed. They came to see previously unheard of places, such as Ladysmith, Mafeking and Kimberley, that now held a special poignancy. They soon realised that southern Africa was also a land of great natural beauty which, thanks to Rhodes' dream of sending a railway from the Cape to Cairo, was now accessible to the visitors.

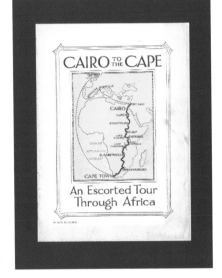

CAIRO TO THE CAPE

An Escorted Tour Through Africa

Work started on a railway out of Cape Town in May 1859, but progress was slow. By 1876, it had only reached Worcester, 109 miles from the Cape, and had progressed only another 230 miles four years later. Then, in 1881, Cecil Rhodes, founder of the De Beers Mining Company, was elected to the Cape Colony Parliament. An avowed imperialist who wished to see the whole map of Africa painted red, Rhodes saw the railway as 'the great civilizer'. Where the railway went, he believed, political and economic control would follow. As prime minister of the Cape Colony from 1890, he backed the relentless northward advance of the iron rails and in 1899 he wrote: 'We propose now to go on and cross the Zambezi just below the Victoria Falls. I should like to have the spray of the water over the carriages.' Rhodes died in 1902, but his hope was realised when the bridge over the Zambezi, one of the most awe-inspiring stretches of railway track in the world, was dedicated on 12 September 1905.

Providing access to an unexplored continent for Cook's tourists had never been Rhodes' intention, but his railway was soon carrying the vanguard of a very different army. Cook, as agent of the Cape Railways, offered a circular tour to the Victoria Falls from Cape Town, with stops at all the major settlements en route. The price in 1907 was £30 4s 9d first class, £21 16s 4d second class.

Although Rhodes failed in his dream of constructing a Cape-to-Cairo railway, Cook's was able to bridge the gap with the firm's Cairo to the Cape Escorted Tour De Luxe. The 11,000-mile journey took three and a half months, with approximately 5000 miles covered by rail, 4000 overland and 2000 by river and lake steamer. The 1936 tour was led by the redoubtable figure of Captain G F Shearwood, formerly of the King's African Rifles, whose services were included in the £590 price tag.

COOK'S
SOUTH AFRICAN
TOURS

OLD STYLE

NEW STYLE

PROGRAMME FREE FROM
THOS COOK & SON
CAPE TOWN CORNER OF STRAND & ST GEORGES STREETS
CHIEF OFFICE: Ludgate Circus London DURBAN SMITH ST.

A TICKET TO RIDE

The world was becoming a smaller place as trains criss-crossed continents and ships plied the oceans. In this 1906 illustration, one of Cook's uniformed representatives shows just how tiny the globe could be thanks to Cook's tickets. (Coloured)

From Brussels to Baghdad, Singapore to Simla, Cook's offices spanned the globe. These branches were the equivalent of the modern travel agent's shop, where customers went to book their holiday, buy tickets and receive advice. Whether located on the Place d'Opera in Paris, Merchant Street in Rangoon or in the grounds of Shepheard's Hotel, Cairo, a dedicated staff, often working from 9 am until 8 pm during the busiest times of year, was on hand to help bring the world to the customer.

When Thomas Cook began his travel business, the infrastructure of tourism was in its infancy: railway lines were few and far between, ships uncomfortable and slow, and hotels expensive and poorly equipped. Cook's main business, therefore, involved escorting groups of excursionists to areas of scenic, historic and cultural interest, such as Scotland and Switzerland.

As Cook's business matured and expanded its horizons, so too did its clientele. The construction of extensive new railway networks, the development of swift and well-appointed steamships and the spread of the grand hotel made the world a more accessible and less threatening place. By 1864, Cook claimed to have one million clients, and by the 1880s over 90 per cent of these were independent travellers. The March 1883 edition of Cook's American *Excursionist* reported: 'We are proud of the fact, that it is almost impossible to get into a railway carriage or on board a steamboat in Europe from May to October and not find one's self in company with passengers traveling on Cook's tickets'.

The great attraction of using Thomas Cook & Son was that, in its capacity as agent to all the major transport companies, it could issue a single ticket for a journey that might necessitate using the services of a dozen different travel providers. Unlike ordinary tickets issued by the various companies, Cook's combination tickets also provided for breaks of journey along the way.

By entering a Cook's office in Chicago, Constantinople or Kobe, the Victorian traveller could book a journey up the Nile, order breakfast on a train to Baghdad or reserve a sedan chair to view the sights of Peking. Cook's frequently emphasised that its brochures only provided a sample of possible routes and, in 1890, during which the firm proudly announced it had sold 3,262,159 tickets, there were over 30,000 different ticket series in existence.

These tickets were issued in a handsome green case. This became the holder's passport to the services of Cook's worldwide network of uniformed representatives and interpreters who were stationed at major stations and ports.

The sale of tickets formed the backbone of Cook's business and the *Excursionist* periodically informed its readers of the rapid growth in numbers. In 1891 the total had reached 3,512,250, in 1897, 5,300,000 and in 1898, on the eve of John Mason Cook's death, 6,650,500 tickets in 40,100 different series were issued covering 2,241,500 miles of railways and waterways.

AT YOUR SERVICE: COOK'S UNIFORMED REPRESENTATIVES

First appearing on the cover of the Far Eastern Traveller's Gazette *in 1933, this picture shows a scene that was repeated at stations and ports around the world: one of Cook's uniformed representatives assists a couple with their onward journey.*

The unique care which Cook's took of its customers did not cease once the journey began. Armed with their tickets, hotel coupons, Circular Notes and guidebooks, Cook's independent travellers were free to roam the globe. There came a time, however, when even the most self-reliant traveller appreciated the help of someone with local knowledge. Starting with the cross-Channel boat trains, Cook's gradually established a worldwide network of representatives and interpreters who were ready to help anyone holding a company ticket.

These representatives were placed at major ports and stations, where the tourist was likely to be in greatest need, and helped customers tackle the awkward first moments in a new country or destination. Thanks to the interpreter's command of languages, expert local knowledge and the requisite unflappability, even the most obstinate or unorganised traveller could be safely helped on their way. Luggage was successfully rounded up, customs negotiated, transport hired or connections made. For ladies travelling alone this facility was considered particularly advantageous. They would be seen 'safely in the trains and their baggage properly checked, thus saving them much petty trouble and annoyance'.

These representatives were dressed in an immaculate uniform of navy blue with gold trim. A peaked cap bore the words 'Thos Cook & Son Ltd', making them immediately recognisable to even the most dazed tourist. Thousands of grateful travellers passed through their hands each year, and they soon acquired considerable local influence. Stories abound of trains being halted and boats delayed on the instructions of one of Cook's uniformed ambassadors, thus allowing a delayed customer to continue their journey as scheduled. The services and assistance of one of these representatives was available free of charge to Cook's customers, though the travel agent warned that they 'are not on duty on Sundays except by special arrangement'.

The Cook's customer to southern Italy was alerted to another danger. 'Most of the guides and commissionaires in the harbour of Naples on offering their services pretend to be Cook's guides. Their [Thomas Cook's] interpreters may always be recognised by the uniform of the firm, and for such only are they responsible'.

By the 1930s, the list of places where Cook's staff met the principal trains and steamers was truly global. It ran the entire alphabet from Algiers to Zeebrugge, with Beirut, Colombo, Dover, Geneva, Hong Kong, Kobe, Milan, New York, Paris, Peking, Shanghai, Southampton, Suez, Venice, Vienna and many more in between.

THE TRAVELLER'S GAZETTE

Cook's new-look Traveller's Gazette *was launched in May 1902, price two pence. This version of the cover was introduced the following year.* (Coloured)

As well as providing the ideal forum for advertising Thomas Cook's tickets, tours and travel services, the *Excursionist*, founded by Thomas Cook in 1851, proved to be a publishing success story. The British edition began slowly, with a circulation of just over 2000 an issue by 1864, and grew steadily. By the time John Mason Cook died in 1899, the print run had soared to 120,000 an issue, with up to half that number of the various foreign editions being produced. Along the way, the publication had also gained in respectability and copies could be found in all the Gentlemen's Clubs of London and at the finest hotels.

Thomas and his son viewed the *Excursionist* as a personal medium through which they could preach the gospel of travel and consequently they both took a keen personal interest in the newsletter's content and design. While they were alive, the newsletter was imbued with their personalities and the resulting idiosyncrasies of its style gave it a unique charm. Their deaths occasioned a complete change. 1902 was a time of transition. Queen Victoria's death the previous year brought to an end the longest reign in the nation's history, an eponymous age that had given rise to Thomas Cook's worldwide excursion business. In May, as the country prepared itself for the coronation of Victoria's son as Edward VII, further proof that this was the end of an era arrived in the post.

The *Excursionist* had been given the Edwardian equivalent of an image change. *Cook's Excursionist and Home and Foreign Advertiser* had been replaced by *The Traveller's Gazette*, *'An Illustrated Journal Devoted to Travel'*. The first issue, date 24 May 1902, laid down the reasons for this dramatic facelift. 'We have felt for a long time . . . that the old title was inappropriate to the high class character of the business of to-day, which embraces the whole civilised world, and enjoys the patronage not only of almost every member of our own Royal Family, but of the Royal Families and Courts of almost every country in Europe, as well as that of their most distinguished subjects'.

The old large-format pages covered with a delightful array of quirky fonts were replaced by smaller sheets sporting a unified typeface, a new layout and a procession of black-and-white photographic images. This was now a corporate journal rather than a personal pamphlet. The contents page of the new *Traveller's Gazette* told its own story. Alongside familiar headings, such as Atlantic sailings, independent tours and hotel coupons, the reader found a new focus on the illustrated travel essay. Early issues, as well as a liberal smattering of articles on the upcoming coronation, contained such delights as 'In Nature's Studio', 'A Typical Yorkshire Dale' and 'The Evolution of the Atlantic Greyhound'.

Although there is far more sense of adventure and romance in turning the pages of an early *Cook's Excursionist* than there ever is in the professionally produced pages of its successor, *The Traveller's Gazette* was written for a contemporary audience and it proved as useful and successful as its predecessor. By the mid 1920s, there were 11 other editions of Cook's *Traveller's Gazette*, all sporting a unified design, a testament to the truly global nature of Cook's business. There were five foreign editions in English: *The American Traveler's Gazette* (New York), *The Australasian Traveller's Gazette* (Melbourne), *The Oriental Traveller's Gazette* (printed in Bombay), *The Malayan Traveller's Gazette* (Singapore) and *The Far Eastern Traveller's Gazette* (Shanghai). The remaining six editions, *La Revue de Voyages* (Paris), *Die Welt-Reise Zeitung* (Vienna/Hamburg), *Cook's Reisblad* (Amsterdam), *La Revista de Viajes* (Madrid), *Cook's Rejse-Tidende* (Copenhagen) and *Rivista di Viaggi* (Rome), were published in French, German, Dutch, Spanish, Danish and Italian respectively. As with so much that was familiar to Thomas Cook, these magazines were brought to a halt by World War II.

THE TRAVELLER'S GAZETTE.

*An Illustrated
Journal
Devoted to Travel*

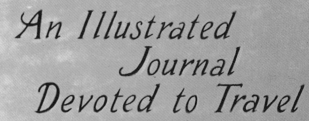

EUROPE
AMERICA · AROUND · COOKS TOURS & ABOUT · ASIA
THE WORLD
AFRICA

Published Monthly
by
THOS COOK & SON

CHIEF OFFICE
LUDGATE CIRCUS, LONDON. E.C.

COSSETED AND CARED FOR

This versatile illustration first appeared in 1903 in The Traveller's Gazette. *The panel lists a selection of destinations for that year's spring tours (e.g. departures for Algeria and Tunisia on 18 March and 22 April, for Italy and the Riviera on 3 and 17 April). Each time the image was reprinted, the list of destinations was updated to reflect the new season's programme.* (Coloured)

Independent travel, Cook's *Excursionist* declared, was all well and good for 'those who have an abundance of time and to whom the cost of the tour is not a special consideration'. For those, on the other hand, whose time or funds were limited, and especially 'ladies and young persons [requiring] some competent and responsible escort', a conducted tour was 'just the thing'.

Thomas Cook & Son prided itself on its long tradition of escorted tours, run to the highest standards and available to almost any part of the globe by the 1900s. 'The entire details of these tours are based upon many years of personal study and experience. The time is divided so as to yield the maximum of benefit and pleasure and the minimum of discomfort. We seek to utilize all the time in the most profitable way and not to waste it, but at the same time allowing a reasonable amount for rest. Our itineraries are so arranged that it is seldom necessary to travel by night, never on Sunday, and tedious journeys are always avoided'.

Participation in one of these organised parties had many advantages. As a matter of economy, it was possible 'to complete any one of the tours . . . without the expenditure of another shilling', while at the same time 'relieving the traveller of all petty troubles and annoyances inseparable from any journey'.

To the socially conscious Victorians, there was another benefit of joining one of Cook's conducted tours. 'The persons joining our parties are uniformly of the most intelligent, refined and cultured class. In fact, it could hardly be otherwise, for the very good reason that persons of any other class would hardly be interested in foreign travel, and would be much more likely to invest any spare money they might have in other ways than in a tour'.

As the size of Cook's business grew, it obviously became impossible for Thomas or his son to escort each group in person. Conductors were vetted and recruited, so that participants could be assured that Cook's representatives were 'persons of experience, familiar with each place visited, having a knowledge of the language of each country and fully qualified to give every necessary information on all points. In many cases members of these parties are admitted to galleries and other places of interest where single travelers might have great difficulty in gaining admission. Rooms in hotels are reserved in advance by the Conductor. Carriages are in waiting at the depot on the arrival of the party and no time is lost in ascertaining what to do or how to do it'.

The majority of the tours on offer explored the familiar regions of Europe and could be as short as one week. At the other end of the scale were trips lasting hundreds of days and travelling to such diverse places as Borneo, Algeria and Cuba.

As a comparison of costs, a circular ticket in 1892 via the main places of interest in Belgium, the Rhine, Switzerland and Paris cost the independent traveller £12 2s first class. A 30-day conducted tour along a virtually identical route cost £42 10s, but as always the conducted tour prices 'are strictly inclusive; that is to say, they provide for railway, steamer and diligence fares, hotel accommodation (with three meals a day); in fact, everything except wine and washing'.

TRAVEL FOR ALL

This 1902 brochure contained the full range of what Cook's called Popular Tours. By combining travel and hotel accommodation for a price that was often less than the cost of an ordinary return ticket they showed that 'it is not necessary to possess a particularly heavy purse in order to visit countries which formerly were visited only by the wealthy'.

What was remarkable about the Cook's organisation was its ability to be all things to all people. By 1902 Cook's had conducted kings and queens, maharajas and princes, presidents and prime ministers to all parts of the globe, and yet Cook & Son never neglected to cultivate the custom of the more prosaic members of society.

The introduction to this 1902 guide makes no bones about its intended market: 'For many people wagon-lits, daily carriage drives, and fashionable and palatial hotels have no attraction, whether from a monetary point of view or from that of comfort'.

The sacrifice does not seem to have been too great, as Cook's idea of a cheap package tour typically consisted of: 'Second-class railway travelling, good comfortable hotels with substantial meat breakfast, good table d'hote dinner in the evening, after a long day's outing, with luncheon of some sort taken wherever happens to be most convenient'. The result was a series of attractively priced Popular Holiday Tours to the most frequently visited areas of Britain and the Continent.

Among the British tours on offer were a week in either Ilfracombe or Lynton, north Devon for £3 12s 6d and packages to a complete range of seaside and health-resort destinations, from Aberystwyth to Yarmouth, comprising third-class rail travel and board and lodging for one week. Example fares from London were: Blackpool 93s 6d (which sounded better than

saying £4 13s 6d), Eastbourne 54s, Scarborough 80s and Weston-Super-Mare 70s.

For the more adventurous, there were tours to France, Germany, Switzerland, Italy and even the offer of a yachting cruise to Norway. A fortnight's tour on 'the large and magnificent' steam yacht *Midnight Sun* was priced at £12 12s (ie 12 guineas). This meant that 'what was formerly the privilege of wealthy persons only, with yachts of their own, is now brought within the resources of people of ordinary means'.

For the majority of the working population, holidays were a rare commodity, a fact the brochure readily acknowledged. An eight-day escorted tour to Geneva, for example, was available for £6 6s with departures every Tuesday from London throughout the summer season. It 'has been organised to meet the wishes of teachers and others who have a limited time at their disposal'.

Another great advantage of Thomas Cook's tours was their flexibility. For those travelling to Geneva who wished to stay in greater comfort and splendour, the brochure offered a one-guinea supplement for accommodation at the luxurious Hotel Metropole; to travel first class as well cost an extra three guineas. On arrival, tourists were free to follow their own schedule or else book one of a number of Cook-run excursions. For those who fancied a stop-over in Paris or Brussels on the way home, there were extension fares available.

MANCHESTER. FIRST EDITION.

HOLIDAY TOURS

SEASON 1902

ORGANISED AND ARRANGED BY

THOS COOK & SON

LONDON, E.C.

LUDGATE CIRCUS,

JOHNSON, RIDDLE, COUCHMAN & Cº LONDON.

INCLUSIVE INDEPENDENT TRAVEL

This Edwardian poster proved to be an adaptable medium for promoting Cook's wide range of travel tickets. It was used over a number of years and updated by simply substituting a more modishly attired group of people standing on the magic carpet and altering the destinations at the genie's feet. (Coloured)

As Cook's grew, it evolved a whole host of ways of catering to the varied needs of its clientele. For those who preferred to travel in a party under the careful supervision of a guide, and have all their arrangements taken care of, Cook's offered conducted tours; for independent travellers, who preferred the freedom to travel when and where they wished, Cook's provided travelling tickets 'to any part of the globe, at any time' and hotel coupons that enabled the traveller to secure accommodation for a fixed sum at a long list of accredited properties. A variation on the independent theme was Cook's Popular Tours. These provided prearranged travel over a set route and accommodation in prescribed hotels for a fare paid in advance. This left room for a further addition to Cook's array of travel options: for individuals or small groups who wished to create a bespoke tour, but wished to avoid the 'worry of details inseparable from independent travel', Cook's devised a system that was termed Inclusive Independent Travel, or IIT.

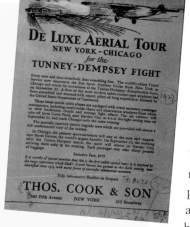

Although small parties had previously taken advantage of this service in all but name, the term IIT only came into currency in the 1900s. This system of 'travel without trouble' was further proof of Cook's remarkable organisational powers. All that was required was an outline of the desired route, however circuitous or unusual, to be submitted to one of Cook's offices. A precise daily itinerary was then drawn up, listing every necessary piece of information, so that 'no more trouble is experienced than is incurred in giving orders to servants at home'.

Armed with this itinerary, produced at great distance from the intended destination and without the benefit of modern communications, the traveller set out to put Thomas Cook & Son to the test. Without fail, IIT travellers found nothing wanting: the train reservations had been secured, they were met on arrival at each stop and transported to and from the hotel where appropriate rooms would be awaiting them on the selected floor. If requested, sightseeing tours and guided tours of places of interest would have been arranged. In all, the *Traveller's Gazette* opined, the tour 'may be said to resemble a series of expected visits to the houses of friends'.

As with a conducted tour, practically every expense, with the exception of 'the bill for beverages and the usual gratuities to hotel servants and porters', was taken care of. The actual cost of this unparalleled service depended on a host of variables, including the number of travellers in the party and the class of hotel selected. As an illustration, Cook's gave the example of a 20-day tour visiting Paris, Genoa, Pisa, Rome, Florence, Venice, Milan, the Italian lakes and Lucerne, with first class travel and accommodation. The fare for a party of four in this instance would be 32 guineas each.

A COOK'S Ticket

LIKE THE MAGIC CARPET

WILL TAKE YOU ANYWHERE YOU WISH

Ludgate Circus, London E.C.

STAYING CLOSE TO HOME

Cook's published a series of guides to its programme of cheap excursions, with titles such as Picnic Tours *and* Day Outings, *often utilising the same cover design. Here a montage of travel images has been used to promote the events planned for the 1911 season.* (Coloured)

By 1911, the whole world was accessible to a Cook's customer with the time and money to enjoy it, but many of Thomas Cook's compatriots had to content themselves with day outings to destinations closer to hand. The term picnic was loosely used to describe any group outing that combined travel, sightseeing and provision of meals along the way. This brochure was aimed primarily at working-class parties wanting to enjoy a fun day out. In this respect, the tours were essentially an updated version of Thomas Cook's very first excursion from Leicester to Loughborough back in 1841. The travel agent, using his bulk purchasing power, was able to offer the tours 'on the most advantageous terms' and to release the group leader from 'the many worries and responsibilities invariably experienced by those who are in the habit of making their own arrangements direct'. Popular destinations included the seaside, beauty spots and sites of historical interest.

As usual with Thomas Cook & Son, flexibility was an inherent feature of its tours. 'Secretaries, organisers and others having the arrangement of Parties' were advised that Cook's welcomed groups 'of any description or size' and was pleased to make arrangements to any chosen resort on receipt of the following information: name of party, name of the place to which travelling and date of picnic, preferred departure and return times, the size of the party, a description of the meals required and at what times, and the drive proposed. It is a tribute to the ethic that Thomas Cook and his son, John Mason Cook, had installed in their firm that, in those precomputer days, the thousands of requests received monthly were dealt with promptly and efficiently.

While offering freedom of choice to those who wanted it, Thomas Cook & Son also quoted in its brochure a list of prearranged tours. To coincide with the ascension to the British throne of George V, a Coronation Exhibition was held in 1911 in Shepherd's Bush, London. For parties of 20–25, or multiples thereof, Cook & Son offered a series of tours to London. For 18s 6d per person, for example, the party, accompanied by one of the company's competent conductors, was provided with return rail tickets to London, a half-day drive around the principal sights, a cooked breakfast and dinner and transport to the exhibition, including admission. Slightly more expensive tours were distinguished by the length and range of the sightseeing tour and, the all-important feature of any picnic, the size and number of meals.

COOK'S
PROGRAMME OF POPULAR
PICNIC TOURS

BY RAIL, COACH, MOTOR & STEAMER.

SAILING THE SEVEN SEAS

Cook's annual Ocean Sailing List *was an essential reference guide to travelling the high seas. This edition, published during the last year of the Great War, heralded the return to peace and business as usual.*

Thomas Cook first took his excursionists to sea in 1846 in order to reach Scotland. In the half century that followed, Cook's established itself as official agents to all the world's major, and many minor, steamship companies, including: the Peninsular & Oriental Steam Navigation Company (which dominated the route to Britain's eastern possessions through the Suez Canal), the Orient, Austrian Lloyd and Pacific Mail lines, the Castle Mail Packet Company, steamers on the Rhine and Danube rivers and, on the high-profile transatlantic run, the Cunard, White Star, Transatlantique and North German Lloyd companies. If a customer wished to cross the Atlantic in state-room luxury, emigrate cheaply to Australia, or ply the waters of the Pacific, hopping from island to island, Cook's Ocean Travel Department could issue the appropriate ticket. Sample prices in this 1918 brochure included: the Union–Castle Line travelled to South Africa with fares to Cape Town ranging from £59 5s for the cheapest first-class cabin to £22 13s for a no-frills third-class berth; the Toyo Kisen Kaisha offered passage to the major cities of the Far East via the United States for £66 10s, with a special missionary rate of £62; and New York to Havana on a United Fruit Company boat was available at £10 8s 4d.

Any of Cook's worldwide network of branches could issue tickets but, for customers booking at a distance, Cook's advised the use of a specially devised telegraphic code. Users were charged by the word when sending telegrams, and so money could be saved by substituting an agreed term for a standard request. Unless stated otherwise, it was always assumed that first-class accommodation was required. *Adhesive*, followed by a number and the name of a ship, was an instruction to book the specified number of gentlemen's berths on the boat mentioned; for women's berths, the term was, in keeping with the times, *Adjutant*. In deference to its pre-eminent status in the east, travel by P&O steamer had its own lexicon: *Addict* for men's berths, *Adder* for women's. In all cases, if Cook's reply was *Gaiter* the required berths had been booked; *Garble* meant that no first-class accommodation was available.

As well as dispensing tickets to all four corners of the globe, Thomas Cook & Son also dispensed advice with 'no charge whatever'. In the introductory section of this 1918 brochure, entitled 'Hints to intending travellers by sea', Cook's noted that 'it is impossible to over-estimate the value of sea travel for the maintenance or the restoration of good health'. Those travelling for pleasure should determine their date of sailing 'by the climatic conditions of the country to be reached'.

Cook's also offered to supply insurance 'upon the lives and effects of Passengers, for any period or voyage, including or not including War risks'. Cover of up to £100 for 14 days, for example, cost 7s 9d.

On routes to North America, Cook's noted, first- and second-class travellers were allowed 20 cubic feet of luggage, steerage class 10 cubic feet, and children and servants baggage in proportion to the fare paid. When deciding what to pack, Cook's suggested 'a sufficiency of woollen underwear to last the voyage and a warm wrap for the deck'.

Cook's warned passengers to beware of thieves on sailing day, to be 'exceedingly careful in entering into any arrangements at home for the purchase of land in foreign countries,' and finally cautioned those left behind against 'the prevalent practice of accompanying departing friends on board the vessel'.

COOK'S OCEAN SAILING LIST.

BOOKINGS
EVERYWHERE
BY ALL THE PRINCIPAL
STEAMSHIP LINES.

THOS COOK & SON,
CHIEF OFFICE :- LUDGATE CIRCUS, LONDON.

FREEDOM OF THE ROADS

Undated, except for the clue given by the design of the car, this poster heralded the arrival of a serious challenge to the dominance of the railways. Cook's saw the automobile's possibilities rather than its long-term threat and lost no time in finding ingenious ways of utilising it for the benefit of its customers.
(Coloured)

Thomas Cook, master of the steam locomotive and liner, died before the internal combustion engine had become a viable addition to the business of travel. Perhaps this was a good thing for, in the long run, the private motor car would help end the railway age and undermine Cook's traditional business of selling tickets. Initially, however, it proved a welcome boon to Cook's enterprise, augmenting rather than replacing the railway.

The problem that had faced Thomas Cook from the earliest days was what to do when the rails ran out. Trains were without doubt the quickest and most comfortable means of travel, but trains only ran where track had been laid. This was fine for the majority of Cook's European tours, which concentrated on urban destinations. It was more of a problem in rural areas, such as Scotland, Ireland and the popular Alpine regions of Italy and Switzerland, where trains either did not or could not go. In these cases, Cook had to resort to a much older form of transport: the horse.

Horse-drawn coaches and diligences were used extensively by Cook's to convey customers to destinations inaccessible by railway and to provide sightseeing tours around cities. But horses were slow, relatively expensive and inappropriate in the more exotic locations, such as Africa and the Far East, that the Cook's organisation was opening up to inquisitive travellers. The arrival of reliable motor transport enabled Cook's to discard this reliance on the horse and to open up previously inaccessible areas to the travelling public.

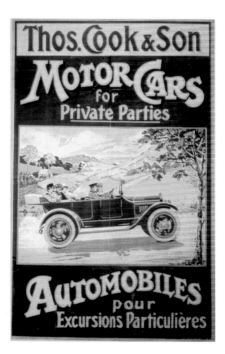

By the 1920s Cook's used a fleet of vehicles, with their own drivers and mechanics, to convey tourists everywhere from the jungles of Malaya to the game reserves of East Africa. The car was also the ideal vehicle for the adventurous. Cook's advised its patrons: 'To those who seek new experiences in travel, there is no more varied or fascinating means of enjoying them than by a tour across Africa by motor . . . We can organize private expeditions of any duration, fully provided with motor transport, white guide, servants, mechanic, stores and all camp equipment'.

The motor car provided the wealthy would-be voyager with the ultimate in flexibility and suitable social cachet to boot. 'Any of our Offices', the *Traveller's Gazette* declared in 1935, 'will be pleased to furnish quotations for the hire of a private car for any itinerary, to suit individual requirements; with or without the services of a uniformed chauffeur, well acquainted with the principal tourist routes; with or without the services of a private courier, of good social standing, who knows thoroughly the usages of the country and is a mine of information about all places visited'.

For those of more limited means, Cook's offered trips by charabanc, an early type of bus. In Britain, it was used on tours of the Lake District and Scotland and this was followed by the first coach tours to the Continent. Sample prices in the 1920s included a five-day tour of the Loire Chateaux for £14 10s and a nine-day exploration of Brittany's less accessible centres for £27 17s 6d.

COOK'S MOTOR HIRE SERVICE

CHAUFFEUR DRIVEN FOR THEATRES . FUNCTIONS . SIGHTSEEING

ONE DAY OR EXTENDED TOURS WITH OR WITHOUT COURIER

"DRIVE YOURSELF" SERVICE — ASK THE BOOKING CLERK.

COOK'S TAKES TO THE AIR

'Have you ever seen the world from the air?' asked the introduction to this 1937 brochure. 'It is a delightful experience and one that never palls'.

The biggest fillip to commercial aviation was provided by World War I. The war necessitated great advances in aeroplane technology and, on the return to peace, aircraft such as the Handley Page bomber were converted for civilian use. The post-war routes linked Europe's major population centres and among the most successful was the London–Paris run.

Planes were still relatively small and a far cry from the luxury that was by then commonplace on the best trains and boats. Make-shift seats were packed into the uninsulated and unheated fuselages, where the noise of the engines made normal conversation impossible. There were no in-flight services and passengers were advised to bring their own hot-water bottles. For those whose stomachs were strong enough to survive the constant buffeting experienced by flying at low altitude, a prepacked lunch box could be purchased for 3s prior to departure. Forced landings were a common occurrence in bad weather and the pilot's main navigational aid was railway lines, with the name of passing stations painted in large white letters on their roofs.

As with any new technology, flying was not initially a cheap option. The fare to Paris from London began at £21, while passengers travelling in comfort via the conventional cross-Channel route paid as little as £3 8s 5d first class.

Despite these drawbacks, flying had one undeniable advantage over existing means of travel: it was quick. With journey times between London and Paris under three hours, compared with a minimum of six and a half hours by boat and train, and the tiresome need to switch between train and boat obviated, the service was particularly appealing to the business traveller. By 1922, over 10,000 passengers a year were using the London–Paris route, and so the airlines turned their attention to improving both the extent of their networks and the level of their service.

Airlines sought to emulate the atmosphere and amenities of the Pullman carriage and luxury liner: the pioneering pilots were replaced by uniformed captains who greeted passengers as they boarded; new purpose-built aircraft incorporated upholstered seating and on-board toilets; and, following the introduction of the first stewards in 1922, customers were served elaborate, multi-course meals.

The formation of larger, national airlines, such as KLM in 1919, Imperial Airways in 1924 and Pan American World Airways in 1928, and further improvements in aeroplane design, including the famous flying boats that were able to land on water, made long-distance air travel possible. Imperial Airways began its first regular service to India in 1926 and to South Africa six years later. As planes still had a limited range, they hopped from airfield to airfield, with passengers accommodated in hotels overnight.

By the time this brochure was printed, Thomas Cook & Son was official agent for 57 of the world's major airlines. The price of a 60-day return ticket from London to Paris had been reduced to £8 (and only £6 15s for a weekend return) and the time to under two hours. Once again Cook's tickets spanned the globe.

Customers could fly from London to Rome on Air France for £13 6s (time 8 hrs 45 mins); Vienna with KLM was £15; Moscow with Deutsche Lufthansa took one and a half days at a cost of £23 6s; and for the ultimate flying experience, Imperial Airways offered twice-weekly departures for Brisbane, at £160 one way, taking 13 days and calling at Marseilles, Rome, Brindisi, Athens, Alexandria, Gaza, Baghdad, Basra, Kuwait, Bahrain, Sharjah, Gwadar, Karachi, Jodhpur, Delhi, Cawnpore, Allahabad, Calcutta, Rangoon, Bangkok, Penang, Singapore, Batavia, Darwin and, finally, Brisbane.

6,000   16/6/37

AIR TRAVEL

COOK'S HANDBOOK OF SERVICES & TOURS 1937

CENTENNIAL EXHIBITION, 1876.

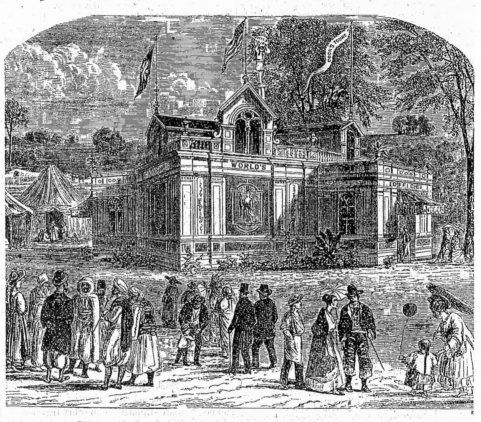

COOK'S WORLD'S TICKET OFFICES,
CENTENNIAL GROUNDS, PHILADELPHIA.

ALL THE WORLD'S A FAIR

The first of two mural paintings by James Dougherty commissioned for the Cook–Wagons-Lits exhibit at the 1939 World's Fair in San Francisco is shown overleaf. The caption over the entrance to the exhibit read: 'The world's oldest and largest travel organisation'. (Coloured)

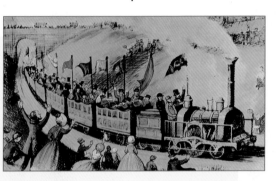

The first World's Fair, held in London's Hyde Park in 1851, proved to be an inestimable boost to Thomas Cook's fledgling excursion business. During the six months the Exhibition was open to the public, Cook made travel arrangements for some 150,000 visitors. It was fitting that an exhibition organised to advertise the advances made by British industry should also provide a showcase for the organisational powers of the Englishman who revolutionised Victorian travel.

National pride and public appetite ensured a procession of increasingly elaborate World Expositions throughout the 19th century, including Paris (1855, 1867, 1878 and 1889), London (1862) and Vienna (1873). Cook had difficulty obtaining travel concessions for the first Paris Expo, but in 1867 20,000 travelled to the Fair with Cook. So-called 'Artizans' Tickets' were available for 'Working men and working women and their Families, on production of a certificate from their Employees'. The return fare, valid for a fortnight, was 27s in second class and 20s in third. Cook also offered four nights' accommodation in a specially rented house for an additional 16s.

Starting with the Vienna Exhibition of 1873, Cook's was appointed passenger agent to the Royal British Commission and at the 1876 Centennial World's Fair in Philadelphia, USA the firm had its own sales outlet, a 'handsome building of wood, hexagonal in form, and sixty feet square' known as The World's Ticket Office. Cook's was proud to announce that this endeavour 'Has been a great centre of attraction, and of public utility. By the aid of an Egyptian princess of the time of the Pharaohs, a mummy of at least 3000 years of age, brought from the Nile last winter by one of our esteemed American tourists, we have given character to our Eastern exhibition of war weapons, Palestine tents, and Jerusalem manufactures; and these features; in connection with half a dozen living representatives of the Holy Land, have daily drawn to our great hall thousands of visitors'. The company also had the honour of making the travel arrangements for Dom Pedro, the Emperor of Brazil, and his party during their visit to the States and the Philadelphia Fair.

The Golden Gate International Exposition of 1939–40 was held on a 400-acre artificial island in San Francisco Bay dubbed Treasure Island. It seems fitting, as the golden era of steam made way for the age of the automobile and aeroplane, that the island was located in the shadow of the Bay Bridge, recently opened to provide a road link with Oakland. There were also plans to turn the island into an airport for San Francisco when the Fair closed, but after the United States of America entered World War II it was taken over by the navy.

Thos Cook & Son Ltd, now owned by Wagons-Lits, chose to adorn its exhibit in the Vacationland Building with two striking murals. The first of these, despite a degree of artistic licence, elegantly traced the early history of the excursion agent from Leicester. In the first panel, filled with the accoutrements of the departing age of stage-coach and inn, Cook's inaugural railway excursion between Leicester and Loughborough is shown steaming into history. The year is 1841.

This is followed by panels depicting some of the milestones in Cook's early expansion – the successful association with the Great Exhibition in 1851, the start of tours on the Continent (which actually began in 1855) and the first visit to Egypt in 1869 – culminating in Cook's inaugural world tour.

1883 EUROPE

THE WAGONS-LITS COMPANY
INAUGURATES THE ORIENT EXPRESS

1884 EGYPT

BRITISH GOVERNMENT
PLACES THOS. COOK & SON IN CHARGE
OF TRANSPORTATION FOR A GREAT
MILITARY EXPEDITION.

FIVE MILLION T
COOK-WAGONS-LITS

TODAY

FRANCE 1918

THE ARMISTICE IS
SIGNED IN A WAGONS-LITS CAR

THE WORLD 1924

ELERS USE
VICES EVERY YEAR

THOS. COOK & SON'S PLEASURE CRUISES
SAIL THE SEVEN SEAS.

A FLIGHT OF FANCY

In 1950, having taken travellers to every point of the terrestrial world over the previous 100 years, Thos Cook & Son Ltd began taking reservations for holidays in space. Here we envisage a Thomas Cook poster from the future.

Leicester to Loughborough was only the beginning. Thomas Cook spent his life expanding the boundaries of travel. Born at a time when steam had yet to be harnessed for the benefit of passenger travel, Cook, by the end of his life, had become the master of every means of modern conveyance. Inspired by the belief that the only way to alleviate the social evil of drinking was to provide an alternative, his excursion business became an extension of his desire to improve the drinker's lot. With almost missionary-like zeal, he constantly sought to tame new destinations and to bring the far-flung corners of this planet within the grasp of the travelling public. Working without the support of a large organisation, and almost entirely without precedent, he devised endless ways to ease the life of travellers the world over, from traveller's cheques to hotel coupons.

In 1841, arranging a short excursion by train was considered a novelty; five years later Cook was breaking new ground by taking a party to the Highlands of Scotland. Another 20 years on and tours of Scotland had became a familiar feature of Cook's annual programme of excursions. Cook had meanwhile crossed the English Channel, mastered the Alps and begun to bring the rest of the continent of Europe within the compass of his tickets and tours.

He was ready for a new challenge. The next region ripe for 'conquest' lay across the capricious waters of the north Atlantic: America. It is easy to forget just how much effort was involved during the infancy of global travel in what would today be a simple undertaking. Cook wrote of his voyage to the United States in 1866: 'The passage was a heavy one, against head winds and a high sea, especially over the banks of Newfoundland . . . On nearing the Bay of New York we were befogged and obliged to cast anchor for about 12 hours'.

First America, then the world. While Jules Verne was creating travel fiction in the shape of *Around the world in 80 days*, Thomas Cook was making travel fact. His inaugural round-the-world trip in 1872–73 was undertaken at a somewhat more leisurely pace than the fictional Phileas Fogg. However, it was still a great testament to Cook's pioneering spirit.

Fast forward to 1950. The firm of Thos Cook & Son Ltd, still imbued with the spirit of its founder, now regularly provided its customers with tickets to all four corners of the globe. It seemed as if the once feared elements of land, sea and air had been brought to order for the benefit of the modern traveller; the journey of weeks had been reduced to one of hours. Inevitably, people began to seek new regions to explore.

In Thomas Cook's day Jules Verne had sent his characters to the moon; in 1950 the subject was tackled by Irving Pichel in *Destination Moon*. The film won an Oscar for best special effects and caught the imagination of Cook's marketing department. To coincide with the film's release Cook's transformed one of its windows at the Berkeley Street headquarters into a space panorama. 'Already the restless mind of man', ran the accompanying text, 'is reaching beyond this little planet, out to the stars. Soon the cold surface of the moon may bear the print of his feet'. At the same time a leaflet was produced advising passengers that 'we are now taking reservations for holidays on the moon and elsewhere in the Solar System'. Thus was born Cook's 'moon register', a list of those interested in booking a place on Cook's inaugural lunar tour, as and when it took place. When men's footprints finally did appear on the moon in 1969, the renewed public interest in the possibilities of stellar travel brought a fresh wave of registrations.

The numbers continued to grow over the years and an official certificate was handed out as proof of membership of this exclusive 'club'. Finally, in November 1996, the register was closed having reached 10,000 names. When the first spaceship will blast off with a contingent of expectant holidaymakers aboard nobody can say. But back in 1950 Cook's reassured its passengers: 'What the future has in store we cannot tell. Of one thing, however, we are certain. We will be there'.

To THE Moon
AND BEYOND
with
Thomas Cook

4⁵ BERKELEY STREET · LONDON W1

The posters and larger images used throughout this book bear captions which explain their place in the history of Thomas Cook and the Golden Age of Travel. A number of items of travel memorabilia have also been used to illustrate this book, and their origins are explained briefly, below.

INDEX OF TRAVEL MEMORABILIA

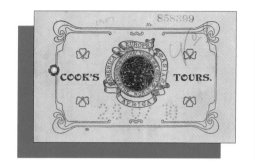

The motif on this ticket has been adapted for use on a number of items of travel memorabilia.

A small selection of posters from the Thomas Cook Archives can be purchased by contacting Thomas Cook Publishing on 01733 503571.

INDEX